Beginning SwiftUI

Greg Lim

Table of Contents

Preface

About this book

In this book, we take you on a fun, hands-on and pragmatic journey to learning iOS 17 development using SwiftUI. You'll start building your first iOS app within minutes. Every section is written in a bite-sized manner and straight to the point as I don't want to waste your time (and most certainly mine) on the content you don't need. In the end, you will have the skills to create an app and submit it to the app store.

In the course of this book, we will cover:
* Chapter 1: Introduction
* Chapter 2: Body Mass Index Calculator
* Chapter 3: To Do List App Using *List*
* Chapter 4: Persistent Data Using Core Data
* Chapter 5: Getting Data from an API: GitHub Users
* Chapter 6: Publishing your App on to the App Store

The goal of this book is to teach you iOS 17 development in a manageable way without overwhelming you. We focus only on the essentials and cover the material in a hands-on practice manner for you to code along.

Requirements

No previous knowledge of iOS development required, but you should have basic programming knowledge.

Getting Book Updates

To receive updated versions of the book, subscribe to our mailing list by sending a mail to support@i-ducate.com. I try to update my books to use the latest version of software, libraries and will update the codes/content in this book. So do subscribe to my list to receive updated copies!

Contact and Code Examples

Contact me at support@i-ducate.com to obtain the source codes used in this book. Comments or questions concerning this book can also be directed to the same.

Chapter 1: Introduction

Welcome to Beginning SwiftUI iOS 17 Development! I'm Greg and I'm so excited that you decided to come along for this. With this book, you will go from absolute beginner to having your app submitted to the App Store and along the way, equip yourself with valuable iOS app development skills.

SwiftUI makes it easier to build user interfaces across all Apple platforms with Swift. It uses a declarative syntax where you simply state what your user interface should do.

Before SwiftUI, developers used UIKit and Storyboard to design user interfaces. We drag and drop UI controls on to View Controllers and connect them to outlets and actions on the View Controller classes. We then update view controls and handle events that occur through delegates. If you would like to learn iOS development using UIKit and Storyboard, check out my best-selling book or contact me at *support@i-ducate.com.*

SwiftUI in contrast is a state-driven, declarative framework. There is no more dragging and dropping in the storyboard. Layouts are specified declaratively using code. For example, you can state that you want a list of items consisting of text views and then describe the value for each view.

```
struct ContentView: View {
    var body: some View {
        List{
            Text("Write SwiftUI book")
            Text("Read Bible")
            Text("Bring kids out to play")
            Text("Fetch wife")
            Text("Call mum")
        }
    }
}
```

Your code is easier to read and write than before, saving you time and maintenance.

Working Through This Book

This book is purposely broken down into brief chapters where the development process of each chapter will center on different essential topics to develop apps for the iPhone. The book takes a practical hands-on approach to learning through practice. You learn best when you code along with the examples in the book. Along the way, if you encounter any problems, drop me a mail at support@i-ducate.com where I will try to answer your query.

Get a Mac

Before we proceed on, you will need to have a Mac running on at least MacOS Sonoma or later to run Xcode 15.

If you do not yet have a Mac, the cheapest option is to get a Macbook Air and if you have a higher budget, get a higher model or iMac with more processing power (I personally use a Macbook Air). You might have heard of the option to run Mac on Windows machines for iOS development, but I do not recommend it. Unexpected problems will arise in development and publishing to the App store that can be avoided by just using a Mac. If you are serious about developing iOS apps and publishing them on the App Store, getting a Mac is a worthwhile investment.

Downloading Xcode

Next, there is an essential piece of software you need to have on your computer before we can move forward. It's called Xcode and is an integrated development environment (IDE) provided by Apple to write Swift code and make iOS apps. It includes the code editor, graphical user interface editor, debugging tools, an iPhone/iPad simulator (to test our apps without real devices) and much more. Let's get it downloaded before proceeding.

Download the latest version of Xcode 15 (at time of writing) from the Mac App Store (fig. 1).

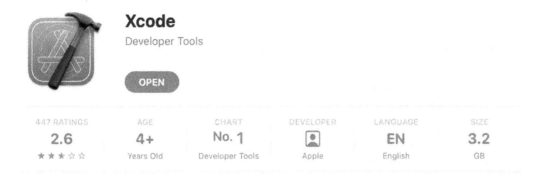

Figure 1

You will need an Apple ID to login and download apps from the Mac App store. If you do not already have one, sign up for an account (https://appleid.apple.com/account). You will also need an Apple ID to deploy your app to a real iPhone/iPad device for testing.

Note: The installation of Xcode might require you to update your version of MacOS.

Installing Xcode

Just like any other Mac App, Mac App store will take care of the downloading and installation of Xcode for you. Do note that installation of Xcode 15 requires 20-30 GB of space available for the installation to proceed and installation takes quite some time. Once the installation is complete, you should see the Xcode icon on your computer.

Swift and Xcode

I'm going to be introducing you to two terms that you're going to encounter throughout this book. One of those is Swift and the other one is Xcode. Swift is the programming language we use to make iPhone apps. Swift came out in 2014. Previous to that, the programming language used to make iPhone apps was Objective C. But Objective C was complicated. Many developers new to the space of iOS development found that it was hard to read and write. Swift then was introduced. Swift is specifically designed with beginners in mind and even experienced programmers think of Swift as a really clean and beautiful language.

Xcode is the program that allows us to make iPhone apps. We're going to type Swift into Xcode and also use Xcode for designing the visual side of our app like where we want a button, what color do we want it to be, where do we want to place our table view, etc.
Throughout this book, these are the two skills that we will be improving upon step by step.

This book is written for a beginner in iOS development. So, you don't need to have any prior iOS development experience. But if you have some iOS development experience, you're going to feel pretty familiar with what's going on.

It will also be best if you have some basic programming experience. But if you do not have it, it's alright and I will try my best to explain certain programming concepts.

Difference between Swift and SwiftUI

In case you are confused about Swift and SwiftUI, Swift is simply the programming language used to build our iOS apps. SwiftUI in contrast is the user-interface side of things where developers create user UIs using Swift in a declarative way. This will become much clearer as we progress along.

Xcode Walkthrough

In this section, I want you to become acquainted with Xcode. Open Xcode.

At the time of writing, this book uses Xcode 15. But make sure you're using the latest official version of Xcode from the Mac App Store.

In the 'Welcome to Xcode' screen (fig. 2), choose 'Create New Project...' where you create a new Xcode project where you create an app for iPhone, iPad, Mac, Apple Watch or Apple TV.

Figure 2

When you do so, it's going to bring up a page (fig. 3) that asks what kind of project do you want to create, whether iOS, watchOS, tvOS, macOS or Multiplatform:

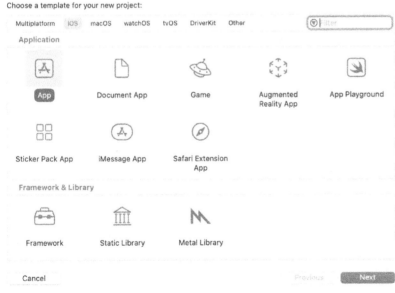

Figure 3

iOS includes apps for the iPhone, iPad, iPod Touch. *watchOS* is for Apple watch apps. *tvOS* is for Apple TV apps. *macOS* is for Mac apps on the desktop and *Multiplatform* is if you want to make an app that works across multiple platforms. For us, we focus on *iOS* apps.

For an iOS app, there are lots of different templates that you can start with. The templates help you get started with some boilerplate code. For us, we want the *App* option. This is essentially the blank starting point for almost every app that we're going to make. So let's go ahead and double click on that.

You will then have to input the below fields for your project (fig. 4):

Product Name: (as this is our first project, we will name it *HelloSwiftUI*)
Team:
Organization Identifier: (normally the reverse of your website e.g. com.iducate.calculator. If you do not have a website, com.firstname.lastname will do fine)
Interface: select *SwiftUI*
Language: select *Swift* (only option available)
For *Storage* and *Include Tests*: leave the boxes unchecked

Product Name:	HelloSwiftUI
Team:	None
Organization Identifier:	com.greglim
Bundle Identifier:	com.greglim.HelloSwiftUI
Interface:	SwiftUI
Language:	Swift
Storage:	None
	Host in CloudKit
	Include Tests

Figure 4

Go ahead and fill in the fields. You can change the field values later in your project, so don't worry if you have inputted a wrong value.

When you have the fields filled up, hit the *Next* button. It's going to ask you where you want to save this new project.

There will also be a checkbox to 'Create Git repository on my Mac'. This will make a GitHub repository for your app which helps you save different versions of your app and if you want to collaborate with people. Git is outside the scope of this book so you can leave it either checked or unchecked.

You should see the project created for you (fig. 5a).

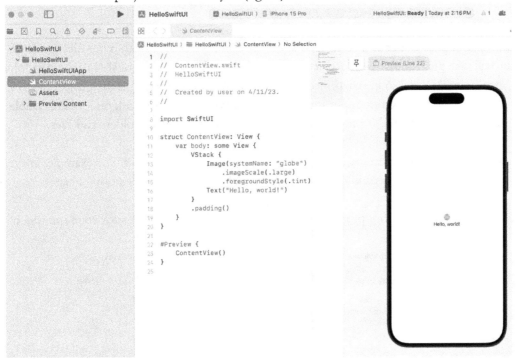

Figure 5a

You can see that a new folder has been added called *HelloSwiftUI*. On the left side of Xcode, you can see the folder-file structure of the project (fig. 5b).

Figure 5b

We have our *HelloSwiftUI* folder at the root and another *HelloSwiftUI* folder with more files inside of that. Xcode will take the name of your project and put that in a folder which consists of another folder with that same name. It will also have a project file *HelloSwiftUI.xcodeproj* which is the project file to open our project. If we close Xcode and wanted to open up your project to work on it again, double click on *HelloSwiftUI.xcodeproj* and it will open up Xcode with all your project folders and files.

And then we have folders like *Assets.xcassets* to store resources that our app uses. For example, images, sounds, fonts, and videos. The apps in this book will have *Assets.xcassets* mainly storing images.

Lastly, if you click back on the root project file, you can see the General settings for your app (fig. 6).

	General	Signing & Capabilities	Resource Tags	Info	Build Settings	Build Phases

PROJECT

HelloSwiftUI

> **Supported Destinations**

∨ **Minimum Deployments**

iOS 17.0

TARGETS

HelloSwiftUI

∨ **Identity**

App Category None

Display Name Display Name

Bundle Identifier com.greglim.HelloSwiftUI

Version 1.0

Build 1

Figure 6

This is where you previously filled in the fields at the beginning of the project. You can come back here and change it.

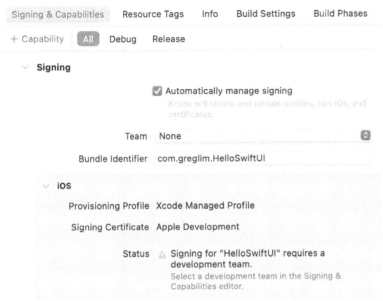

Figure 7

Under the 'Signing & Capabilities' tab (fig. 7) is also where we had to specify the 'Team' field. Again, you can come back here and change it. For example, we have not specified *Team*. Here, you can go back and change when you want to submit your app to the App Store (covered in more detail in the last chapter).

The main file we will work with for now is *ContentView.swift*. *ContentView.swift* contains the UI for our application's initial main screen.

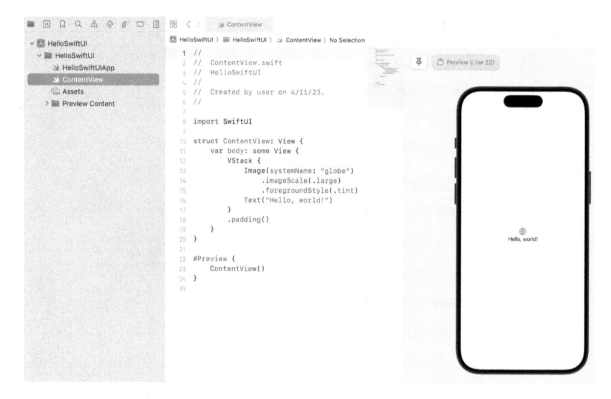

In the above, there is a canvas on the right side of Xcode which lets you preview the UI of your application without needing to run the application on the Simulator or a real device.

ContentView.swift contains the following:

```swift
import SwiftUI

struct ContentView: View {
    var body: some View {
        VStack {
            Image(systemName: "globe")
                .imageScale(.large)
                .foregroundStyle(.tint)
            Text("Hello, world!")
        }
        .padding()
    }
}
```

```
#Preview {
    ContentView()
}
```

Code Explanation

```
struct ContentView: View {
```

The *ContentView* struct defines the UI of your screen. It conforms to the *View* protocol (everything you want to show in SwiftUI needs to conform to *View*). Thus, it must declare a property called *body* which returns some sort of View.

```
var body: some View {
    VStack {
        Image(systemName: "globe")
            .imageScale(.large)
            .foregroundStyle(.tint)
        Text("Hello, world!")
    }
    .padding()
}
```

body currently consists of a *VStack* which in turn contains an *Image* View and a *Text* View. A *VStack* allows us to group different views vertically. We will look at Stacks in depth in a while.

Inside the *VStack*, we have an *Image* View which is a view that displays an image. In our case, it displays a globe image.

Hello, world!

We will dive more into *Image* views later on. We also have a *Text* View which is a view that displays one or more lines of read-only text (in other words, it is a text label).

```
var body: some View {
    ...
}
```

Note: the *some* keyword in the above code literally means "this will return some sort of View but SwiftUI doesn't need to care what."

Try It Out

Change the *systemName* in the *Image* view and the text in the *Text* View as shown below in **bold**:

```
struct ContentView: View {
    var body: some View {
        VStack {
            Image(systemName: "trash")
                .imageScale(.large)
                .foregroundStyle(.tint)
            Text("Hello, SwiftUI!")
        }
        .padding()
    }
}
```

The preview should automatically update to reflect the text change (fig. 9).

Hello, SwiftUI!

Figure 9

Now, what produces the preview? Below the ContentView struct, we have a *#Preview* which produces the previews.

```
...
#Preview {
    ContentView()
}.
```

Although we have introduced previews, to actually run your app, you need to run it on the simulator. To do so, simply click the ▶ icon from the panel on the top left of Xcode:

The simulator should start running and soon display your app.

You can also choose from different simulators to run your app:

Buttons

Other than Texts and Images, Buttons are another visual control that you see in almost all apps. Users click on buttons to call specific code to perform some actions. To add other visual controls, click on '+' on the top right of Xcode:

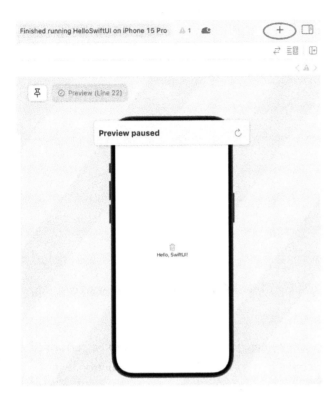

Scroll through the views where you can see how each view is used :

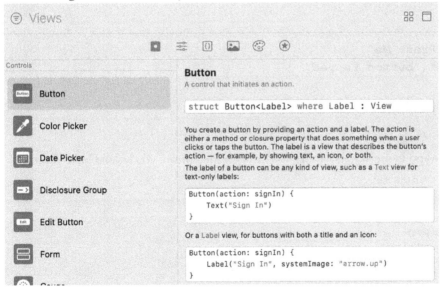

Select 'Button' and click-drag into the code which will auto generate something like the below:

```swift
struct ContentView: View {
    var body: some View {
        VStack {
            Image(systemName: "trash")
                .imageScale(.large)
                .foregroundStyle(.tint)
            Text("Hello, SwiftUI!")
            Button("Button") {

            }
        }
        .padding()
    }
}
```

The *Button* View has a parameter to specify its text e.g. "Button". We will later see how to customize the look of the button with *modifiers*.

In the button code block, you have a parameter *action* where you provide the code to be performed when the button is clicked. Let's add a *print* statement in the action and change the button text:

```swift
struct ContentView: View {
    var body: some View {

        ...

        ...

        Button("Press Me") {
            print("button tapped")
        }

    }
}
```

Now when you run the app in the simulator and you click on the button, you should have "button tapped" printed in the console log.

HelloSwiftUI

```
button tapped
button tapped
```

If your console is not showing, go to 'View', 'Debug Area', 'Activate Console' (fig. 10).

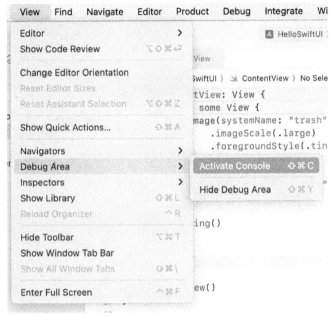

Figure 10

Stacking Views

So far, we have used a VStack to display an Image, Text and a Button. UIs often have multiple and different types of views together. To group and position them, we use stacks. There are three kinds of stacks we can use to group our UI:

VStack - arranges its children views vertically
HStack - arranges its children views horizontally
ZStack - arranges its children views depth based (e.g. back to front)

So, if we want to add a Circle and a Rectangle in the VStack, I would have:

```
var body: some View {
    VStack {
        Image(systemName: "trash")
            .imageScale(.large)
            .foregroundStyle(.tint)
        Text("Hello, SwiftUI!")
        Circle()
        Rectangle()
        Button("Press Me") {
            print("button tapped")
        }
    }
    .padding()
}
```

And this would give me (fig. 11):

Figure 11

Note: by default, a Stack places little or no spacing between two views. But we can control the spacing by providing a parameter when we create the stack:

```
var body: some View {
    VStack(spacing: 20){
        ...
    }
}
```

This will give us slightly more space in between the views:

A VStack also by default aligns its views centered. But we can change that with the 'alignment' property. For e.g.

```
VStack(alignment:.leading){
    ...
}
```

This aligns the views to the leading edge, i.e. aligned left:

Xcode might prompt you with other options available apart from *leading*, for eg. center, trailing.

```
struct ContentView: View {
    var body: some View {
        VStack(alignment:.) {   ⊗  Expected id...
            Image(sys    Ⓜ leading
                .imag    Ⓜ center
                .fore    Ⓜ trailing
            Text("Hel
```

HStack

If I change VStack to HStack:

```
HStack {
    Image(systemName: "trash")
        .imageScale(.large)
        .foregroundStyle(.tint)
    Text("Hello, SwiftUI!")
    Circle()
    Rectangle()
    Button("Press Me") {
        print("button tapped")
    }
}
```

We get (fig. 12):

Figure 12

We can combine VStack, HStack views together to create more complex arrangements. For e.g.:

```
   ...
   HStack{
       ZStack{
           Circle()
               .fill(Color.yellow)
           Button("Press Me") {
               print("button tapped")
           }
       }
       .frame(width: 100.0, height: 100.0)

       VStack(alignment: .leading, spacing: 4) {
           Text("Beginning SwiftUI")
           Text("Greg Lim, 2024")
       }
   }
   ...
```

This gives us (fig. 13):

Beginning SwiftUI
Greg Lim, 2024

Figure 13

Code Explanation

We have a ZStack and a VStack nested in a HStack. The VStack itself contains two Text views. The ZStack contains a circle and a button overlaying the front of it.

We call the *frame* modifier of the ZStack to set its width and height to 100:

```
ZStack{
    Circle()
        .fill(Color.yellow)
    Button("Press Me") {
        print("button tapped")
    }
}
.frame(width: 100.0, height: 100.0)
```

Remember that by default, the views wrapped in a VStack are aligned in the center. We change this with the *alignment* parameter.

```
VStack(alignment: .leading, spacing: 4) {
    Text("Beginning SwiftUI")
    Text("Greg Lim, 2024")
}
```

In our case, we use the *leading* property to align to the left. Other values for alignment are *center* (default) and *trailing*.

Now, how do I know what other parameters or properties are available in SwiftUI? Do I have to memorize all of them? Fortunately, the answer is no. In fact, you can have the above generated for you in Xcode.

For example, to fill in yellow color for the circle, in the code, select the circle and open the 'Attributes Inspector' by going to 'View', 'Inspectors', 'Attributes':

The 'Attributes Inspector' will show on the right:

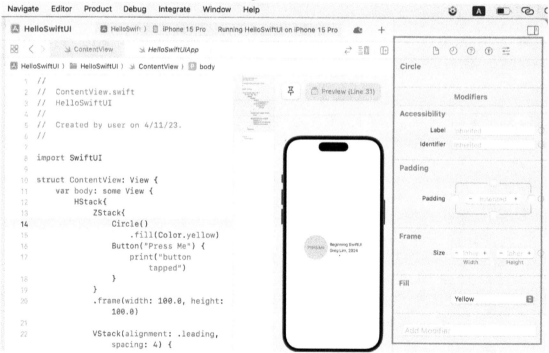

In the 'Fill' modifier in the *Attributes Inspector*, you can then specify the value you want (fig. 14).

It is essentially a WYSIWYG editor where you specify what you want and Xcode will then generate the corresponding Swift code for you.

So suppose I want the text "Beginning SwiftUI" to be larger, I simply select it, and in Attributes Inspector, specify *Font* to be 'Large Title'. And I will get (fig. 15):

Figure 15

Xcode generates the code for me:

```
VStack(alignment: .leading, spacing: 4) {
    Text("Beginning SwiftUI")
        .font(.largeTitle)
    Text("Greg Lim, 2024")
}
```

See how convenient it is?

You can chain specify multiple modifiers to a View also by specifying in Attributes Inspector (fig. 16) (or in the code directly):

which generates the following code:

```
VStack(alignment: .leading, spacing: 4) {
    Text("Beginning SwiftUI")
        .font(.largeTitle)
        .fontWeight(.bold)
        .foregroundColor(Color.gray)
    Text("Greg Lim, 2024")
}
```

Now that we know how to create visual controls from code and buttons to call an action, let's modify our app to create a counter app. A counter app is useful especially when you organize events and want to count the number of attendees. You might have seen a physical one before:

In our counter app, there should be a label which shows how many times the button has been clicked. And each time the button is clicked, the count in the label should be incremented by one. We will then have another button which resets the count to zero. You will also have a variable to store how many times the button has been clicked.

Solution

First, we will need a State variable to store how many times the button has been clicked. Declare a state variable *count* and initialize it to 0 as shown below:

```
struct ContentView: View {

    @State var count: Int = 0

    var body: some View {
        ...
```

Second, we increment *count* by one each time we tap on our button. Let's change "Press Me" to "Increment".

```
    ...
    var body: some View {
        HStack{
            ZStack{
                Circle()
                    .fill(Color.yellow)
                Button("Increment") {
                    self.count += 1
                }
            }
        }
    ...
```

Next, we use String interpolation to display *count*.

```
...
VStack(alignment: .leading, spacing: 4) {
    Text("Count: \(count)")
        .font(.largeTitle)
        .fontWeight(.bold)
        .foregroundColor(Color.gray)
    Text("Greg Lim, 2024")
}
```

The app should look something like (fig. 18):

Count: 0

Greg Lim, 2024

Figure 18

And each time you click on the 'Increment' button, the counter increments by one!

The final code should look like:

```
import SwiftUI

struct ContentView: View {

    @State var count: Int = 0

    var body: some View {
        HStack{
            ZStack{
                Circle()
                    .fill(Color.yellow)
                Button("Increment") {
                    self.count += 1
                }
            }
            .frame(width: 100.0, height: 100.0)
```

```
        VStack(alignment: .leading, spacing: 4) {
            Text("Count: \(count)")
                .font(.largeTitle)
                .fontWeight(.bold)
                .foregroundColor(Color.gray)
            Text("Greg Lim, 2024")
        }
    }
    .padding()
    }
}

#Preview {
    ContentView()
}
```

@State

You might be asking, what is *@State*? The *@State* keyword declares it is a state variable. If a view is dependent on a state variable, SwiftUI ensures that the view is updated whenever the value of the state variable changes. In our case, whenever state variable count changes, the *Text* view `Text("Count: \(count)")` automatically updates to reflect the new value of *count*. We will use State variables throughout the book.

Try it yourself:

Now, can you implement the 'Reset' button functionality which resets count to zero when pressed? Remember to create an action for the reset button and in it set *count* to 0.

Summary

In this chapter, we explained what SwiftUI is and showed how SwiftUI enables us to quickly create user interfaces for our iOS application. We downloaded and installed Xcode and had a walkthrough of the interface. We saw how to layout our views using the two common stacking views, *VStack* and *HStack*. We created our first iOS application using SwiftUI and learned how the various components in our project work together.

Chapter 2: Body Mass Index Calculator

In this chapter, we build a Body Mass Index (BMI) Calculator app. In it, we will reinforce the concepts we have learnt in the previous chapter. We will also learn new concepts like using *TextFields* to get input from users.

If you are unfamiliar with BMI, it helps to see if we are at a healthy weight. To work out your BMI:
- divide your weight in kilograms (kg) by your height in meters (m)
- then divide the answer by your height again to get your BMI

For example: If you weigh 70kg and you're 1.75m tall, divide 70 by 1.75 – the answer is 40 then divide 40 by 1.75 – Your BMI is 22.9.

We then have the following classifications:
Underweight: Your BMI is less than 18.5.
Healthy weight: Your BMI is 18.5 to 24.9.
Overweight: Your BMI is 25 to 29.9.
Obese: Your BMI is 30 or higher.

We will be creating a new project for our BMI Calculator. So, close the current one, and once again go through the steps needed to create a new project: 'Create a New Xcode Project', select 'App', and name your project. I have named my 'BMISwiftUI'. Uncheck all the boxes as we won't be using them yet (fig. 1).

Product Name:	BMISwiftUI
Team:	None
Organization Identifier:	com.greglim
Bundle Identifier:	com.greglim.BMISwiftUI
Interface:	SwiftUI
Language:	Swift
Storage:	None
	Host in CloudKit
	Include Tests

Figure 1

In *ContentView.swift*, we use two TextField views for our weight and height inputs. When you need users to enter some text or numbers, you can use the TextField view.

We also have a Text view that displays "BMI Calculator" on the top. We embed all of them in a VStack.

```
struct ContentView: View {
    @State private var weightText: String = ""
    @State private var heightText: String = ""

    var body: some View {
        VStack{
            Text("BMI Calculator:").font(.largeTitle)
            TextField("Enter Weight (in kilograms)",text: $weightText)
                .textFieldStyle(RoundedBorderTextFieldStyle())
                .border(Color.black)

            TextField("Enter Height (in meters)",text: $heightText)
                .textFieldStyle(RoundedBorderTextFieldStyle())
                .border(Color.black)

        }.padding()
    }
}
```

Code Explanation

```
TextField("Enter Weight (in kilograms)",text: $weightText)
```

The first argument to the TextField view is the placeholder text where we provide hints to the user on how to enter input. In our case, we prompt to the user to enter weight in kilograms e.g. 85 (meaning 85 kg).

```
    @State private var weightText: String = ""
    @State private var heightText: String = ""
```

At the top, we have two private state variables *weightText* and *heightText*. And each of them is bound to the *TextField* object through the *text* parameter.

```
TextField("Enter Weight (in kilograms)",text: $weightText)
TextField("Enter Height (in meters)",text: $heightText)
```

Note that we have the $ prefix to bind the state variable to the view.

When the user types into the TextField, the value of the state variable is updated. Conversely, when we update the state variable, the TextField will also be updated.

Running our App

Let's try running our app in the simulator. You should get something like (fig. 2):

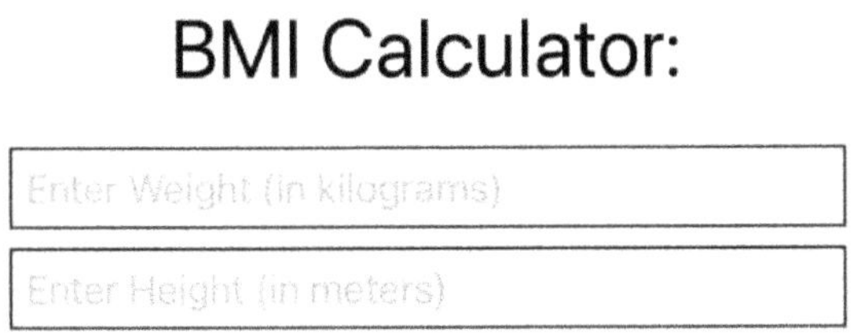

BMI Calculator:

Enter Weight (in kilograms)

Enter Height (in meters)

Figure 2

Modifiers

Notice that we have added some modifiers to our TextField. For e.g.:

```
TextField("Enter Weight (in kilograms)",text: $weightText)
        .textFieldStyle(RoundedBorderTextFieldStyle())
        .border(Color.black)
```

Try removing them and see what happens. For e.g., if you remove *.border*, there won't be any border for the *TextField* and it will be difficult for the user to locate the view.

And *.textFieldStyle(**RoundedBorderTextFieldStyle ()**)* makes the corners of the TextField rounded. With modifiers, we can style *TextFields* (and other views) to our liking.

Calculate and Output BMI Button

Next, we add a "Calculate BMI" button with the following code:

39

```
@State private var weightText: String = ""
@State private var heightText: String = ""
@State private var bmi: Double = 0

var body: some View {
    VStack{
        ...

        Button{
            let weight = Double(self.weightText)!
            let height = Double(self.heightText)!
            self.bmi = weight/(height * height)
        } label:{
            Text("Calculate BMI")
                .padding()
                .foregroundColor(.white)
                .background(Color.blue)
        }

        Text("BMI: \(bmi)").font(.title).padding()
    }.padding()
```

In the above code, because we want to customize our button text's appearance, we pass a custom *label* using a second trailing closure.

And in the button's body, we assign *weight* and *height* with the user inputted value from the TextField. We convert their inputted value from String to Double using *Double(...)* because we will be executing mathematical operations with it.
You might be asking, what is the use of the exclamation mark "!" at the end of the line? We will be explaining this in a section later entitled, "Optionals".

Below the button, we have a Text view that references the state variable *bmi* and displays it so that the user can see it. This is the reason why we have to declare *bmi* as a *@State*. So that when *bmi* changes in value, the Text view recomputes and updates its appearance.

Running our App

When you run your app in the simulator, fill in your weight in kilograms and height in meters (e.g. weight: 85, height: 1.7) and when you click 'Calculate BMI', you have your BMI index printed in the console (fig. 3)! How did you fare? My BMI isn't too good. I had better exercise more!

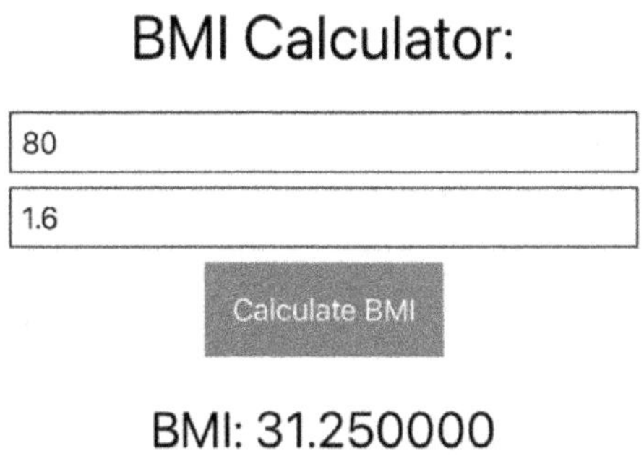

BMI Calculator:

| 80 |
| 1.6 |

Calculate BMI

BMI: 31.250000

Figure 3

Formatting

We should however only display the result to 1 decimal place. To format our result to 1 d.p., we simply add the *specifier* property:

```
Text("BMI: \(bmi, specifier: "%.1f")").font(.title).padding()
```

and our BMI should now display a nicely formatted to 1 d.p. result.

The *specifier* parameter is a specialized string interpolation formatter. "%.1f" is the format code for "floating-point number with one digit after the decimal point".

BMI Classification

Next, we want to append the BMI classification to the BMI for e.g.: "BMI: 29.4, Overweight"

We have to implement the below logic in our Swift code:
Underweight: Your BMI is less than 18.5.
Healthy weight: Your BMI is 18.5 to 24.9.

Overweight: Your BMI is 25 to 29.9.
Obese: Your BMI is 30 or higher.

To do so, add the following code:

```
struct ContentView: View {
    @State private var weightText: String = ""
    @State private var heightText: String = ""
    @State private var bmi: Double = 0
    @State private var classification: String = ""

    var body: some View {
        VStack{
            ...
            ...
            Button{
                let weight = Double(self.weightText)!
                let height = Double(self.heightText)!
                self.bmi = weight/(height * height)

                if self.bmi < 18.5{
                    self.classification = "Underweight"
                }
                else if self.bmi < 24.9{
                    self.classification = "Healthy weight"
                }
                else if self.bmi < 29.9{
                    self.classification = "Overweight"
                }
                else{
                    self.classification = "Obese"
                }
            } label:{
                Text("Calculate BMI")
                    .padding()
                    .foregroundColor(.white)
                    .background(Color.blue)
            }

            Text("BMI: \(bmi, specifier:"%.1f"),\(classification)")
```

```
        .font(.title)
        .padding()


    }.padding()
  }
}
```

Code Explanation

```
@State private var classification: String = ""
```

We first declare a state variable *classification* to store the classification result e.g. Underweight.

```
if self.bmi < 18.5{
    self.classification = "Underweight"
}
else if self.bmi < 24.9{
    self.classification = "Healthy weight"
}
else if self.bmi < 29.9{
    self.classification = "Overweight"
}
else{
    self.classification = "Obese"
}
```

We next then have a series of *if-else* statements to determine the classification as per the BMI classification logic.

```
Text("BMI: \(bmi, specifier:"%.1f"), \(classification)")
    .font(.title)
    .padding()
```

Again, we use Swift string interpolation "\ *(classification)*" to append text before and after the calculated result.

When you run your app now, the BMI classification should be nicely appended to the calculated BMI (fig. 4).

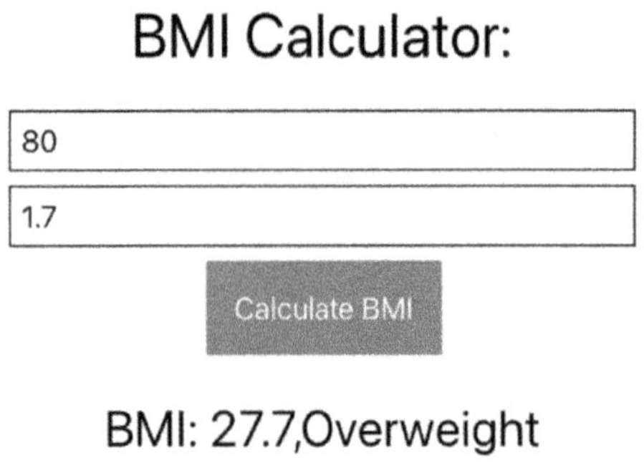

BMI Calculator:

```
80
```

```
1.7
```

Calculate BMI

BMI: 27.7,Overweight

Figure 4

var vs *let*

Now is a good time to revisit our code and look into when we should use *var* and when to use *let*. For example in our code, we declare *weight*, *height* and *bmi* using *let*.

```
let weight = Double(self.weightText)!
let height = Double(self.heightText)!
self.bmi = weight/(height * height)

if self.bmi < 18.5{
    self.classification = "Underweight"
}
    ...
```

But we have declared *classification* using *var*.

The *let* keyword defines a constant, that is, the value won't be changed afterward. In our case, *weight*, *height* after being inputted by the user and *bmi* after being calculated won't be changed, thus we use *let*. We can of course use *var* for these variables and the code will still work.

But it is good practice to use *let* for variables which value never changes. *var* however defines an ordinary variable whose value changes during runtime. For example, *classification* changes during runtime.

Optionals

Earlier, we had the below code with an exclamation mark at the end:

```
let weight = Double(self.weightText)!
let height = Double(self.heightText)!
```

So why do we need it? If you remove the '!', you will get the following error (fig. 6).

```
Button{
    var weight = Double(self.weightText)
    let height = Double(self.heightText)
    self.bmi = weight/(height * height)

    if s
    }
    else
    }
    else
```

❌ Binary operator '*' cannot be applied to two 'Double?' operands

🅞 Value of optional type 'Double?' must be unwrapped to a value of type 'Double'

Coalesce using '??' to provide a default when the optional value contains 'nil'   `Fix`

Force-unwrap using '!' to abort execution if the optional value contains 'nil'   `Fix`

Figure 6

That is, Double(<String>) actually returns a 'Double?' which is a Double optional. In fact, any variable type with a '?' as suffix will make an existing type an optional. This is to specify that either this variable has a value, or it is nil. For example, *Double?* would either have a double value or nil. *Int?* would either have an integer value or nil.

You might ask, why should `Double(self.weightText)` return an optional? Shouldn't it just return a double? Now when a user enters a string such as "Hello World", this cannot convert into a double. So, when a value cannot be converted into a double, it returns nil.

Therefore, `Double(self.weightText)` returns an optional, that is, it returns the double value entered by the user and returns nil when the user does not enter anything in the textfield or enters an incompatible value e.g. letters.

To unwrap an optional, i.e. get the value directly, we add "!" as a suffix to a variable. But as you might have guessed, it is quite dangerous to do so especially when there's the possibility that our variable indeed has a nil value. In fact, if you run the BMI calculator app and leave the field blank and calculate BMI, the app will crash with an error like:

"Fatal error: Unexpectedly found nil while unwrapping an Optional value"

To avoid our app crashing when a textfield is left blank, we should unwrap the optional using '*if let*'. '*if let*' first checks if an optional variable contains an actual value and bind the non-optional form to a temporary variable. This is the safe way to "unwrap" an optional or in other words, access the value contained in the optional.

```
...

Button{
    if let weight = Double(self.weightText),
        let height = Double(self.heightText),
      height != 0 {
        self.bmi = weight / (height * height)

        if self.bmi < 18.5{
            self.classification = "Underweight"
        }
        else if self.bmi < 24.9{
            self.classification = "Healthy weight"
        }
        else if self.bmi < 29.9{
            self.classification = "Overweight"
        }
        else{
            self.classification = "Obese"
        }
    }
    else{
        // show error message
        self.classification = "Invalid input"
    }
} label:{

    ...

}
```

In the above code, we are saying, only move forward if `Double(self.weightText)` is not nil (i.e. it's a valid double numerical value) and in such a case, assign the value double to temporary variable *weight* (*weight* does not exist outside the scope). We then do the same for height. Additionally, we also check for *height != 0* to avoid an invalid division by zero.

Summary

In this chapter, we illustrated the basic structure of a SwiftUI view through the *Text* view and *Button* view. We were introduced to input views which allow us to collect input from users. Applying that knowledge, we went to create a Body Mass Index calculator app. In the next chapter, we will explore how to use *List* views in our app.

Chapter 3: To Do List App Using List

In this chapter, we will be building the classic To-Do app where you have a list of to-dos in a List view (fig. 1). The List view is a container that displays rows of items.

In this chapter and the next, we will see how to dynamically populate a list, add todos to a list, remove todos from a list, as well as edit todos in the list:

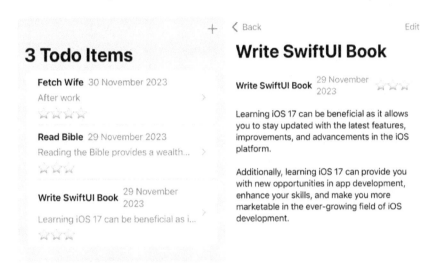

First, begin a new 'App' project in Xcode, call it *TodoSwiftUI*. Under 'Language' choose 'Swift', under 'Interface' choose 'SwiftUI'.

Leave 'Storage' as None. We won't be using Swift Data for now, but we will implement it in the next chapter for data persistency.

To have a List view displaying a list of to-dos, enter the following code in *ContentView*:

```
struct ContentView: View {
    var body: some View {
        List{
            Text("Write SwiftUI book")
            Text("Read Bible")
            Text("Bring kids out to play")
            Text("Fetch wife")
            Text("Call mum")
        }
    }
}
```

When the preview updates, you will see the five rows of text in a list:

Write SwiftUI book

Read Bible

Bring kids out to play

Fetch wife

Call mum

Currently, each row displays a single Text view. But we can put more views together to display more information.

Let's use the *VStack* together with *HStacks* to have each row contain the todo title, todo date, todo note, and stars to indicate level of importance:

Write SwiftUI book 11-11-2023
We can explore the fundamentals of S...
☆☆☆☆☆

Read Bible 11-11-2023
The Bible is a religious text that contain...
☆☆☆☆☆

Bring kids out to play 11-11-2023
It's a great idea to bring the kids out to...
☆☆☆☆☆

To illustrate, I will show the code for the first two rows and you can go ahead to duplicate for subsequent rows:

```
var body: some View {
    List{
        VStack(alignment: .leading){
            HStack{
                Text("Write SwiftUI book").bold()
                Text("11-11-2023")
                    .foregroundStyle(.secondary)
            }
            .padding(.bottom,1)
            HStack{
                Text("We can explore the fundamentals of SwiftUI,
                    including views, data flow, and animations.")
                    .lineLimit(1)
                    .foregroundStyle(.secondary)
            }
            .padding(.bottom,1)
            HStack{
                Text(String(repeating:" ",count: 5))
            }
        }
        VStack(alignment: .leading){
            HStack{
                Text("Read Bible").bold()
                Text("11-11-2023")
                    .foregroundStyle(.secondary)
            }
            .padding(.bottom,1)
            HStack{
                Text("The Bible is a religious text that contains
                    various books and teachings of Christianity.")
                    .lineLimit(1)
                    .foregroundStyle(.secondary)
            }
            .padding(.bottom,1)
            HStack{
                Text(String(repeating:" ",count: 5))
            }
```

```
        }
      }
   }
```

Code Explanation

```
    List{
        VStack(alignment: .leading){
            HStack{
                ...
            }
            .padding(.bottom,1)
            HStack{
                ...
            }
            .padding(.bottom,1)
            HStack{
                ...
            }
        }...
    }
```

In our List, each todo row is represented by a VStack which contain three HStacks.

Fetch Wife 30 November 2023

After work   >

☆☆☆☆

The contents of the VStack are aligned to the left with *VStack(alignment: .leading)*.

```
    HStack{
        Text("Write SwiftUI book").bold()
        Text("11-11-2023")
            .foregroundStyle(.secondary)
    }
    .padding(.bottom,1)
```

In the first HStack, we have a text view to contain the todo title in bold. We then have a second text view to display the date with a secondary foreground style to make it appear less prominent:

Write SwiftUI book 11-11-2023

We can explore the fundamentals of S...

☆ ☆ ☆ ☆ ☆

We add a *.padding(.bottom,1)* to the bottom of the HStack to have some padding from the next HStack below.

The second HStack in each VStack contains a Text view with the todo note string:

Write SwiftUI book 11-11-2023

We can explore the fundamentals of S...

☆ ☆ ☆ ☆ ☆

```
HStack{
    Text("We can explore the fundamentals of SwiftUI,
        including views, data flow, and animations.")
        .lineLimit(1)
        .foregroundStyle(.secondary)
}
.padding(.bottom,1)
```

The *.lineLimit(1)* modifier is used to limit the text to a single line. We show the full note in a detail view later on. Again, *.foregroundStyle(.secondary)* is used to make the note less prominent.

```
HStack{
    Text(String(repeating:"⭐",count: 5))
}
```

The third HStack in the VStack contains a Text view that repeats a star emoji ("⭐") five times, which indicates the importance level for the task.

Populating Rows from an Array

Currently, we have a static list view with hardcoded pieces of fixed data. Let's now see how to populate each row with values from an array.

Because each row consists of todo title, date, note and importance, we will create a *Class* to store them.

Classes allow us to create complex data types that are made up of multiple values. We can then create an instance of the class and fill in its values to pass it around our code.

Todo Class

In *ContentView.swift* at the top, add:

```
import SwiftUI

final class Todo {
    var title: String
    var note: String
    var importance: Int = 1
    var date: Date = Date()

    init (title: String, note: String, importance: Int, date:Date){
        self.title = title
        self.note = note
        self.importance = importance
        self.date = date
    }
}
...
```

We have defined a *Todo* Class that contains four properties:

var title: String to store the title of the to-do item.

var note: String to store the todo note (additional information about the to-do item)

var importance: Int = 1 represents the importance or priority of the to-do item, with a default value of 1. The property type is set to be Integer, i.e. least importance being '1', most important being '5'.

var date: Date = Date() holds a date value, defaulted to the current date and time. It's initialized with *Date()*, which creates a new Date object representing the time the Todo was created.

Array of Todo Structs

Next, declare a state array of Todo objects in *ContentView.swift*:

```
struct ContentView: View {

    @State private var todos = [
        Todo(title: "Grocery Shopping",
            note: "Need to buy vegetables and fruits.",
            importance: 3,
            date:Date()),
        Todo(title: "Read a Book",
            note: "Finish reading 'The Swift Programming Language'",
            importance: 2,
            date:Date()),
        Todo(title: "Workout",
            note: "Go for a 30-minute run in the park",
            importance: 1,
            date:Date())
    ]
            ...
```

We use a state variable *todos* so that the items in the List view can be updated dynamically. Notice how Swift makes it easy to create instances of our *Todo* Class. We simply pass in initial values for *title, note, importance* and *date*.

Next, fill in the below into *body*:

```
    var body: some View {
        List{
            ForEach(todos,id:\.date){(todo) in
                VStack(alignment: .leading){
                    HStack{
                        Text(todo.title).bold()
                        Text(todo.date, style:.date)
                            .foregroundStyle(.secondary)
                    }
                    .padding(.bottom,1)
                    HStack{
                        Text(todo.note)
                            .lineLimit(1)
                            .foregroundStyle(.secondary)
                    }
                    .padding(.bottom,1)
                    HStack{
```

```
            Text(String(repeating:"★",
                    count: todo.importance))
                }
            }
        }
    }
}
```

In the List view, we use a *ForEach* which receives an array and then creates multiple subviews. We have to supply *id* to uniquely identify each item. For now, we supply *.date* to use the todo date as the identifier for each row (since the date includes time/seconds and will be unique).

When you preview your app, it should show the same as before, only this time, your rows are populated programmatically from the *todos* array:

Grocery Shopping 6 November 2023
Need to buy vegetables and fruits
★ ★ ★

Read a Book 6 November 2023
Finish reading 'The Swift Programming...
★ ★

Workout 6 November 2023
Go for a 30-minute run in the park
★

Displaying the List within a NavigationStack

We will next implement a todo details screen. That is, when a user taps on a todo, we will go to a separate todo details screen. We achieve this by wrapping our List in a *NavigationStack*.

```
var body: some View {
    NavigationStack{
        List{
            ForEach(todos,id:\.date){(todo) in
                ...
                ...
            }
        }.navigationTitle("\(todos.count) Todo Items")
    }
}
```

We set the title in the navigation bar using the *navigationTitle* method. Notice that the *navigationTitle* modifier belongs to the *List* view and not to the *NavigationStack*. This is because *NavigationStack* displays new screens by pushing them on top. Each screen has its own title. If the title is attached to the Navigation Stack, the title is fixed. By attaching the title to what's inside the NavigationStack, the title can change as its content changes.

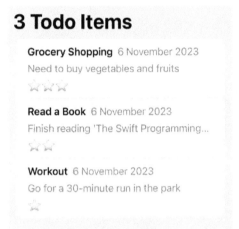

As you can see, a navigation title (listing the count of todo items) has been added to the top of our List (fig. 6).

Navigating to TodoDetailsView

Wrapping the List view in a NavigationStack allows us to navigate to another page when a row is tapped. Let's first create a TodoDetailsView.

Select 'File', 'New', 'File...':

Under 'User Interface', select 'SwiftUI View':

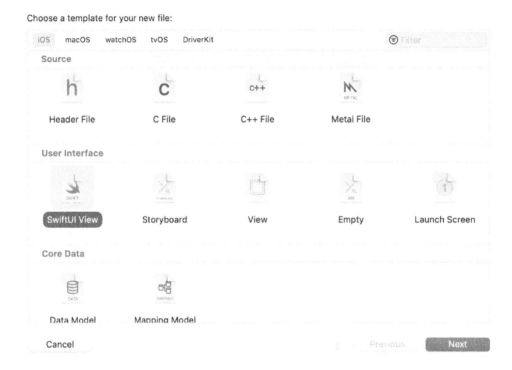

Name the view 'TodoDetailsView' and click 'Create'.

In *TodoDetailsView*, fill in the following:

```
import SwiftUI

struct TodoDetailsView: View {
    let detailTodo: Todo

    var body: some View {
        VStack{
            HStack{
                Text(detailTodo.title).bold()
                Text(detailTodo.date, style:.date)
                    .foregroundStyle(.secondary)
                Text(String(repeating:"☆",count: detailTodo.importance))
            }
            Text(detailTodo.note)
        }
    }
}

#Preview {
    TodoDetailsView(detailTodo: Todo(title: "Sample Task",
                                    note: "This is a sample note.",
                                    importance: 3,
                                    date: Date()))
}
```

Code Explanation

The above code defines a SwiftUI view named *TodoDetailsView* to display details of a to-do item.

```
struct TodoDetailsView: View {
    let detailTodo: Todo
```

We have a constant *detailTodo* of type Todo which contains the details of the to-do item to be displayed. *detailTodo* will be provided when the user clicks on a row in the Todos list and creates an instance of TodoDetailsView. We will implement that shortly.

```
var body: some View {
    VStack{
        HStack{
            Text(detailTodo.title).bold()
            Text(detailTodo.date, style:.date)
                .foregroundStyle(.secondary)
            Text(String(repeating:" ",count: detailTodo.importance))
        }
        Text(detailTodo.note)
    }
}
```

Inside a VStack, there is an HStack which contains:
- *detailTodo.title* in bold font.
- *detailTodo.date* displayed using the built-in *.date* style, which formats the date appropriately.
- A Text view that creates a string repeating the " " emoji *detailTodo.importance* times
- Following the HStack, there is another Text view that displays *detailTodo.note*, which contains additional notes about the to-do item.

To allow previewing of how our TodoDetailsView will look like, we have a dummy todo instance unde #Preview:

```
#Preview {
    TodoDetailsView(detailTodo: Todo(title: "Sample Task",
                                    note: "This is a sample note.",
                                    importance: 3,
                                    date: Date()))
}
```

This gives us something like:

Sample Task 6 November 2023

       This is a sample note.

NavigationLink

Now, back in the List view of ContentView, wrap the row item in a *NavigationLink* function:

```
var body: some View {
    NavigationStack{
        List{
            ForEach(todos,id:\.date){(todo) in
                NavigationLink(destination:
                    TodoDetailsView(detailTodo: todo)){
                    VStack(alignment: .leading){
                        HStack{
                ...
        }
                    }
                }
            }
        }.navigationTitle("\(todos.count) Todo Items")
    }
}
```

In *NavigationLink*, we create an instance of *TodoDetailsView* and provide *todo* as an argument to it.

When you run your app and tap on an item, the selected todo details will be presented on the TodoDetailsView. The top bar in the new screen will also show 'Items' with a back symbol:

⟨ 3 Todo Items

Grocery Shopping 6 November 2023 ⭐⭐⭐
Need to buy vegetables and fruits

Improvements

The todo details view isn't too nice though. Let's improve it so that the todo title is listed on top and

61

the text can be shifted more to the top. We will also add a scroll view when the to-do note is very long, the user can scroll to read. To do so, in *TodoDetailsView*, add in **bold**:

```
struct TodoDetailsView: View {
    let detailTodo: Todo
    var body: some View {
        ScrollView{
            VStack(alignment: .leading){
                HStack{
                    Text(detailTodo.title).bold()
                    Text(detailTodo.date, style:.date)
                        .foregroundStyle(.secondary)
                    Text(String(repeating:" ",count:
                        detailTodo.importance))
                    Spacer()
                }
                .padding(.bottom)

                Text(detailTodo.note)
            }
            .padding()
        }
        .navigationTitle(detailTodo.title)
    }
}
```

Our Todo details view will now look something like:

‹ Back

Grocery Shopping

Grocery Shopping   6 November 2023   ★ ★ ★

Need to buy vegetables and fruits. I suggest visiting a local grocery store or farmers market to purchase a variety of fresh vegetables and fruits.They often have a wide selection of locally sourced produce that is both tasty and nutritious. You can also consider checking online grocery delivery services, as they offer convenience and a wide range of fresh produce options at your fingertips.

Summary

In this chapter, we have built the classic 'To Do List' app. We showed how to display a list of items using a *List* view, a container that displays rows of items in a single column. We explained how to dynamically populate a List and navigate to a Todo's Detail view. In the next chapter, we will implement adding, removing, editing todos, and how to keep all these persistent (i.e. the changes persist even when we close and open the app again)

Chapter 4: Persistent Data Using SwiftData

In this chapter, we will be using Swift Data to keep our data persistent i.e., we will be able to save our to-do items and retrieve them even after we close and open our app. SwiftData allows us to take the objects we have created and saved them into an internal database. We later retrieve the objects from the database when we need to.

SwiftData is a persistence framework built for Swift. It was announced at WWDC23. Previously, we had to use CoreData for data persistency, but SwiftData is built on top of CoreData and is much simpler to set up and work in your app. So let's begin applying Swift Data to your project.

Don't worry if you did not specify 'Swift Data' under 'Storage' when you created the project. We will add the usage of Swift Data into our existing project from scratch.

Creating our SwiftData Model

Creating our SwiftData Model is straightforward. We already have our Todo class which we turn into a SwiftData model by simply adding:

```
import SwiftUI
import SwiftData

@Model
final class Todo {
    var title: String
    var note: String
    var importance: Int = 1
```

```
    var date: Date = Date()

    init (title: String, note: String, importance: Int, date:Date){
      ...
    }
}
```

SwiftData requires the use of Classes for models. We *import SwiftData* and apply the *@Model* macro to add *Todo* to our SwiftData schema. *Todo* model will then be part of the schema and its properties will be persisted using SwiftData.

Model Container

Having created our Todo model, we have to make our *Model Container* available to our app. We do so by adding to *TodoSwiftUIApp.swift*:

```
import SwiftUI

@main
struct TodoSwiftUIApp: App {
    var body: some Scene {
        WindowGroup {
            ContentView()
        }
        .modelContainer(for: [Todo.self])
    }
}
```

The *ModelContainer* creates and manages the actual database file for SwiftData's storage needs, so that the system knows where to read and write data persistently. If you have used Core Data previously, it is the same as *NSPersistentContainer*.

Now that the *ModelContainer* has been setup, we can start using SwiftData with SwiftUI.

Setting up a SwiftUI View with SwiftData

ContentView.swift

Next in *ContentView.swift*, make the changes in **bold**:

```
...
struct ContentView: View {
    @Environment(\.modelContext) private var modelContext
    @Query private var todos: [Todo]

    @State private var todos = [
              ...
          Todo(title: "Workout", note: "...", importance: 1, date:Date())
      ]
    ...
```

Code Explanation

```
@Environment(\.modelContext) private var modelContext
```

With the *@Environment* variable, we establish a context to access our Model Container. Model Context tracks all objects that have been created, modified and deleted in memory, so they can be saved to the Model Container at some later point (improves performance since we don't have to read/write every time we use a piece of data i.e. make a whole bunch of changes in memory and save to storage in one pass).

```
@Query private var todos: [Todo]
```

We use another Swift Macro called *@Query* to load *Todo* models into our view. Now, all *Todos* that exist in our container can be accessed through *todos* which acts as a list.

We thus delete the previous hardcoded dummy todos array:

```
@State private var todos = [
              ...
          Todo(title: "Workout", note: "...", importance: 1, date:Date())
      ]
```

We are no longer using them since we are using Swift Data.

The rest of the code stays the same i.e. where we display todos in the List. We currently have not created

67

any Todos yet, so *todos* will be empty for now. So let's try adding a Todo.

Adding a New Todo

To add rows to our List view, we add a new todo item to the *todos* array. We will use the Tool bar item in the *NavigationStack* for adding *todos*. Add in **bold**:

```
var body: some View {
    NavigationStack{
        List{
            ForEach(todos,id:\.date){(todo) in
                ...
                ...
            }
        }
        .navigationTitle("\(todos.count) Todo Items")
        .toolbar{
            ToolbarItem{
                Button(action:{
                    let newTodo = Todo(title: "title 1",
                                       note: "note 1",
                                       importance: 4,
                                       date: Date())
                    modelContext.insert(newTodo)
                }){
                    Label("Add Todo", systemImage:"plus")
                }
            }
        }
    }
}
```

Code Explanation

```
NavigationStack{
    List{
            ...

            ...

    }
    .navigationTitle("\(todos.count) Todo Items")
    .toolbar{
        ToolbarItem{
            Button(action:{
```

In the NavigationStack, we define a ToolbarItem within a *.toolbar* modifier. Inside the ToolbarItem, there's a Button view which performs an action when tapped. The action is defined in a closure passed to the *action:* parameter:

```
    .toolbar{
        ToolbarItem{
            Button(action:{
                let newTodo = Todo(title: "title 1",
                                   note: "note 1",
                                   importance: 4,
                                   date: Date())
                modelContext.insert(newTodo)
            }){
                Label("Add Todo", systemImage:"plus")
            }
        }
    }
```

Inside the button's *action* closure, we create a new instance of Todo with some hardcoded values (we will later change this) and insert it into *modelContext* `modelContext.insert(newTodo)`.

The button is labeled "Add Todo" and uses a 'plus' system image:

Running our App

Run your app now and when you tap on '+', a new todo item is added to the List view (fig. 10).

Figure 10

AddTodoView

Our current new todo's title and note is hard-coded as "title 1" and "note 1" which shouldn't be the case.

We should instead have a *AddTodoView* presented for users to add a todo. Create our *AddTodoView* by going to 'File', 'New', 'File…':

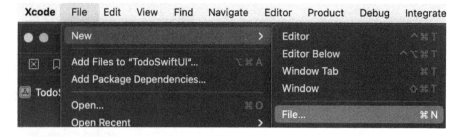

Choose 'SwiftUI View':

Click 'Next' and name it 'AddTodoView':

A new *AddTodoView.swift* file will then be created for you:

```
import SwiftUI

struct AddTodoView: View {
    var body: some View {
        Text("Hello, World!")
    }
}

#Preview {
    AddTodoView()
}
```

Back in *ContentView*, add the below line:

```
struct ContentView: View {
    @Environment(\.modelContext) private var modelContext
    @Query private var todos: [Todo]

    @State var showAddTodoView = false

    var body: some View {
        NavigationStack{
          ...
          ...
```

We have a state variable *showAddTodoView* to determine if we should show *AddTodoView*. It is initially defaulted to false (not showing).

Next, add the below codes in **bold**:

```
            ...
            ...
            .navigationTitle("\(todos.count) Todo Items")
            .toolbar{
                ToolbarItem{
                    Button(action:{
                        showAddTodoView = true
                        let newTodo = Todo(title: "title 1",
                                            note: "note 1",
                                            importance: 4,
                                            date: Date())
                        modelContext.insert(newTodo)
                    }){
                        Label("Add Todo", systemImage:"plus")
                    }
                }
            }
            .sheet(isPresented: $showAddTodoView){
                AddTodoView()
            }
            ...
            ...
```

Code Explanation

```
            Button(action:{
                showAddTodoView = true
                let newTodo = Todo(title: "title 1",
                                    note: "note 1",
                                    importance: 4,
                                    date: Date())
                modelContext.insert(newTodo)
            }){
                Label("Add Todo", systemImage:"plus")
            }
```

In the button's action, we set *showAddTodoView* to true.

```
.sheet(isPresented: $showAddTodoView) {
    AddTodoView()
}
```

To display the sheet, we use the *sheet* modifier and attach it to the List view. We bind *showAddTodoView* state variable to the *isPresented* parameter of the *.sheet()* modifier. When *showAddTodoView* is true, the sheet is displayed over the List view:

Let's next add text fields to specify a new todo and a *Add* button that when clicked, adds the todo and programmatically dismisses the screen.

Adding User Inputs

Let's add user inputs for a user to add a new todo in AddTodoView:

Cancel	New Todo	Save

Title

Date   29 Nov 2023

Enter note...

73

First, add the below into *AddTodoView*:

```
import SwiftUI
import SwiftData

struct AddTodoView: View {
    @Environment(\.modelContext) private var modelContext
    @Environment(\.dismiss) var dismiss

    @State var title: String = ""
    @State var note: String = "Enter note..."
    @State var importance: Int = 1
    @State var date: Date = Date()

    var body: some View {
        Text("Hello, World!")
    }
}
```

Code Explanation

```
@Environment(\.modelContext) private var modelContext
@Environment(\.dismiss) var dismiss
```

Again, we have the Model Context to track objects that have been created, modified and deleted in memory, so they can be saved to the Model Container at some later point. We will discuss *dismiss* later on.

```
@State var title: String = ""
@State var note: String = "Enter note..."
@State var importance: Int = 1
@State var date: Date = Date()
```

We have four state properties to store the *title*, *note*, *importance* and *date* of the todo item.

NavigationStack with Form

Next, in AddTodoView, in *body,* we add a NavigationStack containing a Form with input controls. Add the below code:

```
var body: some View {
    NavigationStack{
        Form {
            TextField("Title", text: $title)
            DatePicker("Date",
                    selection: $date,
                    displayedComponents: .date)
            TextEditor(text: $note)
        }
        .navigationTitle("New Todo")
        .toolbar{
            ToolbarItem(placement: .navigationBarLeading) {
                Button("Cancel") {
                    dismiss()
                }
            }
            ToolbarItem(placement: .navigationBarTrailing) {
                Button("Save") {
                    let newTodo = Todo(title: title,
                                    note: note,
                                    importance: importance,
                                    date:date)
                    modelContext.insert(newTodo)
                    dismiss()
                }
            }
        }
    }
}
```

Code Explanation

```
var body: some View {
    NavigationStack{
        Form {
```

We use a Form within a NavigationStack to create the user interface and functionality for creating a new to-do item. The NavigationStack allows us to add buttons to navigate back to the List of todos by clicking on either 'Cancel' or 'Save':

Cancel	**New Todo**	Save

Title

Date   14 Nov 2023

Enter note...

```
Form {
    TextField("Title", text: $title)
    DatePicker("Date",
            selection: $date,
            displayedComponents: .date)
    TextEditor(text: $note)
}
.navigationTitle("New Todo")
.toolbar{
        ...
}
```

Form is a container that groups our TextField, DatePicker and TextEditor user input control in an organized way.

TextField("Title", text: $title): A text field for the user to enter the title of the to-do item. The $*title* binding means that any text input by the user will be stored in the *title* state property.

DatePicker("Date", selection: $date, displayedComponents: .date): A date picker for the user to select a date. It's bound to the *date* state property and only displays the date component (not time).

TextEditor(text: $note): A text editor for longer text input, used here for entering a note. It's bound to the *note* state property.

```
Form {
...
}
.navigationTitle("New Todo")
.toolbar{
    ToolbarItem(placement: .navigationBarLeading){
        Button("Cancel"){
            dismiss()
        }
    }
    ToolbarItem(placement: .navigationBarTrailing){
        Button("Save"){
            let newTodo = Todo(title: title,
                               note: note,
                               importance: importance,
                               date:date)
            modelContext.insert(newTodo)
            dismiss()
        }
    }
}
```

With *.toolbar*, we add a toolbar to the navigation bar. Inside this toolbar are two ToolbarItem instances.

Cancel	New Todo	Save
Title		
Date	14 Nov 2023	
Enter note...		

```
ToolbarItem(placement: .navigationBarLeading){
    Button("Cancel"){
        dismiss()
    }
}
```

We have the 'Cancel' ToolbarItem placed on the left side with `placement: .navigationBarLeading`. Pressing this button calls the *dismiss()* function, which dismisses the current view.

```
ToolbarItem(placement: .navigationBarTrailing){
    Button("Save"){
        let newTodo = Todo(title: title,
                            note: note,
                            importance: importance,
                            date:date)
        modelContext.insert(newTodo)
        dismiss()
    }
}
```

The 'Save' ToolbarItem is placed on the right side of the navigation bar with `placement: .navigationBarTrailing`.

When pressed, it creates a new *Todo* object with the current values of title, note, and date. We will get to 'importance' later.

We then insert this new Todo object into our data store *modelContext* and call *dismiss()* to close the view.

Running our App

Cancel   **New Todo**   Save

Finish up iOS 17 Book

Date   14 Nov 2023

Learning iOS 17 can be beneficial as it allows you to stay updated with the latest features, improvements, and advancements in the iOS platform.

Additionally, learning iOS 17 can provide you with new opportunities in app development, enhance your skills, and make you more marketable in the ever-growing field of iOS development.

When we run our app and click on '+', the AddTodoView shows up with a form for creating a new to-do item, allowing the user to enter a title, select a date, and write a note. It has a navigation bar with "Cancel" and "Save" buttons for dismissing the view or saving the new to-do item.

After adding the todo, it will show up in the List:

Finish up iOS 17 Book   14 November 2023

Learning iOS 17 can be beneficial as i...   >

☆

Sorting

We have a current issue here where the most recent todo gets added to the bottom of the list. Say I want to order the todos such that the most recent todo is at the top of the list, I can sort by specifying in *ContentView.swift* (where I list my todos):

```
struct ContentView: View {
    @Environment(\.modelContext) private var modelContext
    @Query(sort:\Todo.date, order: .reverse) private var todos: [Todo]
    ...
```

In *@Query*, we specify *sort:\Todo.date* to indicate that the fetched data should be sorted based on the *date* property of the Todo, and *order: .reverse* specifies that the sorting should be in reverse order, meaning it will sort starting from the most recent date.

When you run your app now, the todos are listed according to most recent being first:

Updating in SwiftData

We are currently able to add new todos. Let's now see how we can edit an existing todo in SwiftData. Create a new SwiftUI view file (in Xcode, 'File', 'New', 'File') called EditTodoView:

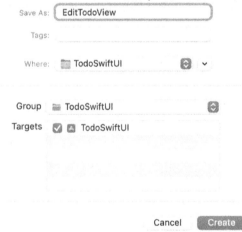

*We have done this before, so it should be familiar.

In *EditTodoView*, add in the following code:

```
import SwiftUI
import SwiftData

struct EditTodoView: View {

    @Environment(\.modelContext) private var modelContext
    @Environment(\.dismiss) var dismiss

    @State var editingTodo: Todo
    @State var editMode = false

    var body: some View {
        Text("Hello, World!")
    }
}
```

The usage of *modelContext* and *dismiss* is the same as in *AddTodoView*.

We have *@State var editingTodo: Todo* which declares a state variable *editingTodo* that represents the current to-do item to be edited.

We have *@State var editMode = false*. *editMode* is used to toggle between different UI modes in the view. If its true, we show the EditTodoView and if its false, we show the DetailTodoView. Let's go ahead and do it now.

In EditTodoView, add in **bold**:

```
struct EditTodoView: View {

    @Environment(\.modelContext) private var modelContext
    @Environment(\.dismiss) var dismiss

    @State var editingTodo: Todo
    @State var editMode = false

    var body: some View {
```

```
        if editMode {
            ...
        } else {
            TodoDetailsView(detailTodo: editingTodo)
                .toolbar {
                    Button("Edit") {
                        editMode = true
                    }
                }
        }
    }
}
```

When *editMode* is false, we just show TodoDetailsView. We also show an 'Edit' button in the toolbar which when pressed, sets *editMode* to true.

‹ 3 Todo Items   Edit

Read Bible

Read Bible 29 November 2023 ⭐⭐⭐

Reading the Bible provides a wealth of knowledge, insight, and guidance for those seeking spiritual understanding and moral principles in their lives.

---

*If you get an error with your preview, you can provide a dummy todo to EditTodoView:

```
#Preview {
    EditTodoView(editingTodo: Todo(title:"sample task",
                                   note: "sample note",
                                   importance:3,
                                   date: Date()))
}
```

Running our App

Before we can run our app, we have to do a minor change in *ContentView.swift*:

```
var body: some View {
    NavigationStack{
        List{
            ForEach(todos,id:\.date){(todo) in
                NavigationLink(
                    destination: EditTodoView(editingTodo: todo)){
                    //destination: TodoDetailsView(detailTodo: todo)){
                    VStack(alignment: .leading){
                        ...
                        ...
```

Instead of showing TodoDetailsView, we show EditTodoView (which in turn shows TodoDetailsView). Now when we run our app, click on a specific todo, we get the TodoDetailsView as before:

‹ Back   Edit

Finish up iOS 17 Book

Finish up iOS 17 Book   14 November 2023

Learning iOS 17 can be beneficial as it allows you to stay updated with the latest features, improvements, and advancements in the iOS platform.

Additionally, learning iOS 17 can provide you with new opportunities in app development, enhance your skills, and make you more marketable in the ever-growing field of iOS development.

But how about when we click on 'Edit' (ie. *editMode* is true)? Let's implement that next.

Implementing Edit and Delete

Let's now implement the code when *editMode* is true. Add in the codes in **bold**:

```
var body: some View {
    if editMode {
        Form {
            TextField("Title", text: $editingTodo.title)
            DatePicker("Date",
                        selection: $editingTodo.date,
                        displayedComponents: .date)
            TextEditor(text: $editingTodo.note)
                .frame(minHeight: 200)
        }
        .navigationTitle("Edit Mode")
        .toolbar {
            Button("Delete") {
                modelContext.delete(editingTodo)
                dismiss()
            }
            .foregroundColor(.red)
            Button("Done") {
                editMode = false
            }
        }
    } else {
        TodoDetailsView(detailTodo: editingTodo)
            ...
    }
}
```

Code Explanation

```
Form {
    TextField("Title", text: $editingTodo.title)
```

We again use the Form view to build a form for editing a to-do item. Like the Form in AddTodoView, it includes a TextField for editing the title. Because it is binded to the *title* property of the *editingTodo* object, the TextField will be pre-populated with its existing value. And as the user makes changes in the text field, the *title* property is automatically updated. The same applies for the DatePicker and TextEditor:

```
DatePicker("Date",
            selection: $editingTodo.date,
            displayedComponents: .date)
TextEditor(text: $editingTodo.note)
    .frame(minHeight: 200)
```

Note that we add a .frame(minHeight: 200) modifier to the TextEditor to show multiple lines of text for longer notes:

```
.toolbar {
    Button("Delete") {
        modelContext.delete(editingTodo)
        dismiss()
    }
    .foregroundColor(.red)
    Button("Done") {
        editMode = false
    }
}
```

We have a toolbar containing two buttons, 'Delete' and 'Done'.

When the 'Delete' button is tapped, it calls *modelContext.delete(editingTodo)* to delete the current *editingTodo* item from the data model, and then calls *dismiss()* to dismiss the view.

We use the modifier *.foregroundColor(.red)* to set the text color of the "Delete" button to red, a common UI indication for a destructive action.

When the 'Done' button is tapped, it sets the *editMode* state variable to false, and we display the TodoDetailsView instead of the EditTodoView.

Running your App

When you run your app, you can edit and also delete existing todo items.

Specifying a Todo's Importance Using Sliders

Lastly, we finish up our Todo app by allowing a user to specify the level of importance for a todo when adding or editing (its currently hardcoded):

The user will use a slider to specify the importance of a todo: [sceenshot]

But we meet with a problem where the slider only accepts a Double type, whereas *importance* is an Integer type. Thus, we have to change *importance* to a *Double*. In ContentView, change:

```
@Model
final class Todo {
    var title: String
    var note: String
    var importance: Double = 1
    var date: Date = Date()

    init (title: String, note: String, importance: Double, date:Date) {
      ...
    }
}
```

In the *NavigationStack*, add in **bold**:

```
    var body: some View {
        NavigationStack{
```

```
List{
    ForEach(todos,id:\.date){(todo) in
        NavigationLink(
            destination: EditTodoView(editingTodo: todo)){

            VStack(alignment: .leading){
                ...
                HStack{
                    Text(String(repeating:"✗",
                        count: Int(todo.importance)))
                }
            }
        }
    }
}
```

Since *count* accepts only an Integer, we have to cast a Double into an Integer.

In *AddTodoView*, make the changes in **bold**:

```
struct AddTodoView: View {
    ...

    @State var title: String = ""
    @State var note: String = "Enter note..."
    @State var importance: Double = 1
    @State var date: Date = Date()

    var body: some View {
        NavigationStack{
            Form {
                TextField("Title", text: $title)
                DatePicker("Date",
                    selection: $date,
                    displayedComponents: .date)
                Text(String(repeating:"✗",count: Int(importance)))
                Slider(value: $importance, in: 1...5, step: 1)
                TextEditor(text: $note)
                    ...
```

By binding to the *importance* state variable, the Slider displays both the current value of *importance* and update it as the user interacts with the Slider. *importance* should be Double or Float since Slider works with floating-point values.

in: 1...5 defines the range of the slider. The slider's minimum value is 1 and its maximum value is 5. *step: 1* defines the step increment of the slider. Since it's set to 1, the slider will move in increments of 1. This means the slider can only take on the whole number values 1, 2, 3, 4, or 5 to set the level of importance of a todo.

And in TodoDetailsView, change:

```
struct TodoDetailsView: View {
    let detailTodo: Todo

    var body: some View {
        ScrollView{
            VStack(alignment: .leading){
                HStack{
                    Text(detailTodo.title).bold()
                    Text(detailTodo.date, style:.date)
                        .foregroundStyle(.secondary)
                    Text(String(repeating:"⭐",
                        count: Int(detailTodo.importance)))
                    Spacer()
                }
                ...
```

When you run your app and add a todo, you can specify the level of importance now using the slider.

88

Changes to EditTodo

Lastly, in EditTodoView, make the changes similar to what we did in AddTodoView:

```
struct EditTodoView: View {

    ...

    var body: some View {
        if editMode {
            Form {
                TextField("Title", text: $editingTodo.title)
                DatePicker(...)
                Text(String(repeating: " ",
                            count: Int(editingTodo.importance)))
                Slider(value: $editingTodo.importance, in: 1...5, step: 1)
                TextEditor(...)
            }
```

And you are now able to edit the importance level of a todo.

Chapter 5: Getting Data from an API: GitHub Users

In this chapter, we will learn how to connect our app with the Internet. We will be connecting to an API to get the data of GitHub users.

Start a new 'App' project and name it 'GitHubUsers'. Choose the options for SwiftUI as we have done before. As we won't be using Swift Data, leave 'Storage' as 'None'.

GitHub RESTful API

We will illustrate by connecting to the GitHub RESTful API to retrieve and manage GitHub content. You can know more about the GitHub API at

```
https://docs.github.com/en/free-pro-team@latest/rest
```

But as a quick introduction, we can get GitHub users data with the following url,

```
https://api.github.com/search/users?q=<search term>
```

We simply specify our search term in the url to get GitHub data for user with name matching our search term. An example is shown below with search term *greg*.

```
https://api.github.com/search/users?q=greg
```

When we make a call to this url, we will get the following json objects as a result (fig. 1).

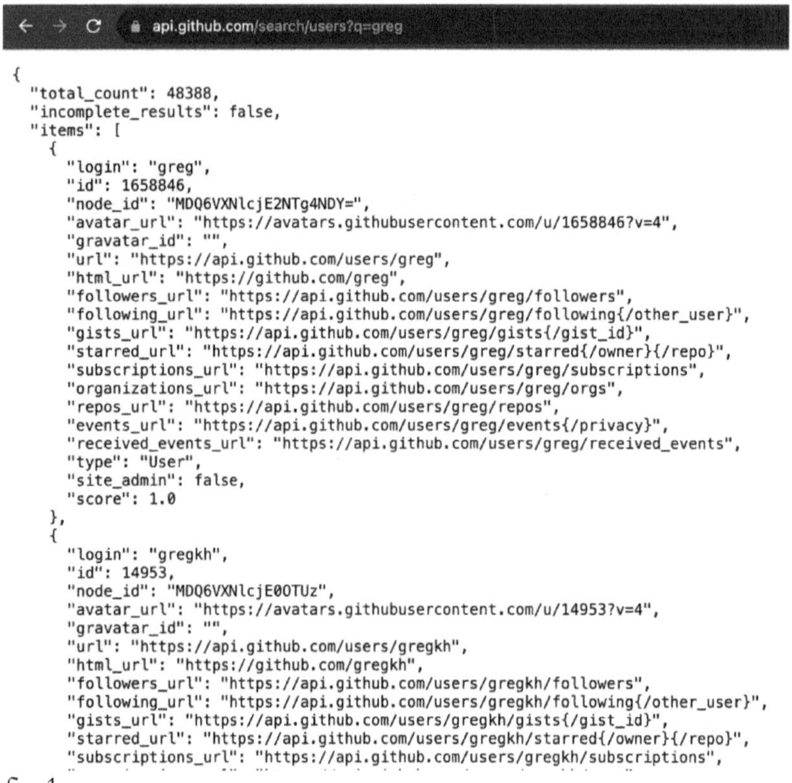
api.github.com/search/users?q=greg


```
{
  "total_count": 48388,
  "incomplete_results": false,
  "items": [
    {
      "login": "greg",
      "id": 1658846,
      "node_id": "MDQ6VXNlcjE2NTg4NDY=",
      "avatar_url": "https://avatars.githubusercontent.com/u/1658846?v=4",
      "gravatar_id": "",
      "url": "https://api.github.com/users/greg",
      "html_url": "https://github.com/greg",
      "followers_url": "https://api.github.com/users/greg/followers",
      "following_url": "https://api.github.com/users/greg/following{/other_user}",
      "gists_url": "https://api.github.com/users/greg/gists{/gist_id}",
      "starred_url": "https://api.github.com/users/greg/starred{/owner}{/repo}",
      "subscriptions_url": "https://api.github.com/users/greg/subscriptions",
      "organizations_url": "https://api.github.com/users/greg/orgs",
      "repos_url": "https://api.github.com/users/greg/repos",
      "events_url": "https://api.github.com/users/greg/events{/privacy}",
      "received_events_url": "https://api.github.com/users/greg/received_events",
      "type": "User",
      "site_admin": false,
      "score": 1.0
    },
    {
      "login": "gregkh",
      "id": 14953,
      "node_id": "MDQ6VXNlcjE0OTUz",
      "avatar_url": "https://avatars.githubusercontent.com/u/14953?v=4",
      "gravatar_id": "",
      "url": "https://api.github.com/users/gregkh",
      "html_url": "https://github.com/gregkh",
      "followers_url": "https://api.github.com/users/gregkh/followers",
      "following_url": "https://api.github.com/users/gregkh/following{/other_user}",
      "gists_url": "https://api.github.com/users/gregkh/gists{/gist_id}",
      "starred_url": "https://api.github.com/users/gregkh/starred{/owner}{/repo}",
      "subscriptions_url": "https://api.github.com/users/gregkh/subscriptions",
```


fig. 1

Note that the value of the *items* key is an array of users, each containing the details of each user. In each user, we want to retrieve the following:
login – User's GitHub login
url – User's GitHub json url
avatar_url – User's avatar image
html_url - User's GitHub webpage

Structs

In *ContentView.swift*, create the following structs:

```swift
import SwiftUI

struct Result: Codable{
    var items: [User]
}

struct User: Codable{
    public var login: String
    public var url: String
    public var avatar_url: String
    public var html_url: String
}

struct ContentView: View {

    ...

    ...

}
```

Both structs conform to the *Codable* protocol so that we can later pass them to JSON Decoder to decode the JSON response string back into the respective structs.

Why do we need two separate structs? We use the *Result* struct to encapsulate the first level of the JSON results:

```json
{
  ...
  "items": [
    {
      "login": "greg",
      ...
    },
    {
      "login": "gregkh",
      ...
    },
  ...
}
```

We specify that we just want access to the *items* property, which is an array of *User* objects. We then define the *User* struct with the properties that we want from the JSON results.:

```json
{
  ...
  "items": [
    {
```

```
      "login": "greg",
      "id": 1658846,
      "avatar_url": "…",
      "url": "https://api.github.com/users/greg",
      "html_url": "https://github.com/greg",
      …
    },
    {
      "login": "gregkh",
      …
    },
  …
}
```

In our case, we have just accessed two levels of the JSON response, *items* and its property, *users*. But there is no limit to the number of levels Codable can go through. Just ensure that your structs should match the JSON structure.

Also, note that the variable names have to be exactly like in the JSON file. For e.g. it has to be strictly *avatar_url* instead of *avatarUrl*.

Fetching Users

Next in ContentView.swift, create a function *getUsers* and a state variable *users* with the following code:

```
struct ContentView: View {
    @State var users: [User] = []

    var body: some View {
        ...
    }
```

```
func getUsers() {
    if let apiURL = URL(string:
        "https://api.github.com/search/users?q=greg") {
        var request = URLRequest(url: apiURL)
        request.httpMethod = "GET"
        URLSession.shared.dataTask(with: request) {
            data, response, error in
            if let userData = data {
                if let usersFromAPI =
                    try? JSONDecoder().decode(
                        Result.self, from:userData) {
                    users = usersFromAPI.items
                    print(users)
                }
            }
        }.resume()
    }
}
```

Code Explanation

```
struct ContentView: View {

    @State var users: [User] = []

    var body: some View {
        ...
    }
}
```

We have a *users* array to store the decoded JSON User content from the API. As mentioned earlier, the @State property wrapper indicates that *users* is part of the view's state, and any changes to it will cause the view to re-render.

```
func getUsers() {
    if let apiURL = URL(string:
        "https://api.github.com/search/users?q=greg") {
        var request = URLRequest(url: apiURL)
        request.httpMethod = "GET"
```

getUsers is responsible for fetching user data from the GitHub API. It starts by constructing a URL with a query parameter *q=greg* to search for users on GitHub whose usernames contain "greg". We hardcode this for now but will later provide a search box for users to specify their own search terms.

A URLRequest is then created with this URL, and the HTTP method is set to "GET", as our request is for retrieving data.

```
URLSession.shared.dataTask(with: request) {
    data, response, error in
    ...
}.resume()
```

We then input the URL request into *URLSession.shared.dataTask* which creates the task for calling a web service endpoint on a remote server. *URLSession* is used to create the session. With the session, we then call *dataTask* to create a data task.

URLSession.shared.dataTask expects us to provide a completion handler which is the function that gets called when the request completes. When the request completes, we are provided with the data retrieved, the response and any errors thrown.

```
URLSession.shared.dataTask(with: request) {
    data, response, error in
    if let userData = data {
        if let usersFromAPI =
            try? JSONDecoder().decode(
                Result.self, from:userData) {
            users = usersFromAPI.items
            print(users)
        }
    }
}.resume()
```

In the completion handler function, we check if any data was received (*if let userData = data*), in which case, our request got connected successfully and we proceed to retrieve the data.

When the JSON content is downloaded, we use the *JSONDecoder()* object's *decode()* function to decode the JSON content into the *Result* struct we defined earlier. When the conversion is done, we assign the result to the *users* variable.

If the decoding is successful, the *users* array is updated with *usersFromAPI.items*, which contains the list of user objects fetched from the API:

```
{
  "total_count": 48390,
  "incomplete_results": false,
  "items": [
    {
      "login": "greg",
      "id": 1658846,
      "node_id": "MDQ6VXNlcjE2NTg4NDY=",
      "avatar_url": "https://avatars.githubusercont
      "gravatar_id": "",
      "url": "https://api.github.com/users/greg",
```

```
URLSession.shared.dataTask(with: request) {
    data, response, error in
    ...
}.resume()
```

Finally, *.resume()* is called on the task to start the network call. Network tasks are created in a suspended state; calling *resume()* actually fires off the task.

List View to Display Users

Next, we will use a List view in a *NavigationStack* to display the list of users we've just retrieved:

```
struct ContentView: View {
    @State var users: [User] = []

    var body: some View {
        NavigationStack {
            List(users, id: \.login) { user in
                VStack(alignment: .leading) {
                    Text(user.login)
                    Text("\(user.url)")
                        .font(.system(size: 11))
                        .foregroundColor(Color.gray)
                }
            }
        }
        ...
```

The List view is bound to the *users* array and we use a VStack to display the user's GitHub login id and url.

Fetching of Data and Showing a Loader Icon

While getting content from a server, it is often useful to show a loading icon to the user .

In *body* of *ContentView*, we check if *users.count* has no items (indicating that retrieval is still in progress). If so, show the *ProgressView* and call *getUsers()* in the *ProgressView*'s *.onAppear()* (lifecycle method called when the view appears).

```
var body: some View {
    NavigationStack {
        if users.count == 0 {
            VStack{
                ProgressView().padding()
                Text("Fetching Users...")
            }
            .foregroundStyle(Color.purple)
            .onAppear{
                getUsers()
            }
        }
        else{
            List(users, id: \.login) { user in
                ...
                ...
                ...
            }
        }
    }
}
```

After data is loaded, *users* will be populated. The view will be notified since *users* is a State variable and the List view will show the objects in *users*.

When you run your app now, it will show the progress view while data is being loaded (it will only appear for a split second).

Here's how the app looks like when you run it (fig. 2):

Figure 2

Display Images Remotely

So far, we have displayed our GitHub users data nicely in a List view. Next, we will explore how to show the user's avatar image.

To load images remotely and asynchronously, we make use of *AsyncImage*. Add the codes in **bold**:
…
…
```
List(users, id: \.login) { user in
    HStack(alignment: .top){
        AsyncImage(url:URL(string:user.avatar_url)){response in
            switch response{
            case .success(let image):
                image.resizable()
                    .frame(width: 50, height: 50)
            default:
                Image(systemName: "nosign")
            }
        }
```

```
        VStack(alignment: .leading) {
            Text(user.login)
            Text("\(user.url)")
                .font(.system(size: 11))
                .foregroundColor(Color.gray)
        }
    }
}
```

Code Explanation

```
    HStack(alignment:.top){
```

Inside the List, each user is represented by a horizontal stack (HStack). We show the GitHub user image horizontally left of the user details with content aligned to the top. This means that if the elements inside the HStack have different heights, they will be aligned such that their top edges are in line.

```
    AsyncImage(url:URL(string:user.avatar_url)){response in
        switch response{
          ...
        }
    }
```

Within the HStack, *AsyncImage* is used to asynchronously load and display an image from the URL stored in *user.avatar_url*.

The *AsyncImage* initializer starts a download task and provides a closure to handle the response. The closure receives a parameter called *response*, which represents the result of the image loading operation.

```
        switch response{
```

The closure uses a *switch* statement to handle different outcomes of the image loading process.

```
    AsyncImage(url:URL(string:user.avatar_url)){response in
        switch response{
    case .success(let image):
        image.resizable()
            .frame(width: 50, height: 50)
    default:
        Image(systemName: "nosign")
    }
```

```
            }
```

If the image is successfully retrieved (*case* *.success*), it is made *resizable* (allowing it to be resized to fit within the given frame) and then assigned a frame with a fixed width and height of 50 points each. This means the image will display as a 50x50 pixel square.

If the image fails to load for any reason (e.g., network issues, invalid URL, etc.), a default system image with the symbol name "nosign" is displayed instead. The "nosign" symbol is one of the symbols provided by SF Symbols, which can represent an error or absence of content.

When you run your app, the avatar image is displayed next to their details (fig. 4).

Figure 4

Wrapping each User in a Link View

Next, we implement that upon tapping a row, we will be brought to the GitHub webpage of the user in a web browser. The GitHub page url is stored in the *html_url* property of the *User* struct. So, add the below:

```
...
List(users, id: \.login) { user in
    Link(destination: URL(string: user.html_url)!){
        HStack(alignment: .top){
            AsyncImage(url:URL(string:user.avatar_url)){response in
                switch response{
                    ...
                }
            }
            VStack(alignment: .leading) {
                ...
            }
        }
    }
}
...
```

When you run the app, tap on a row and the user's web page will be loaded in the web browser:

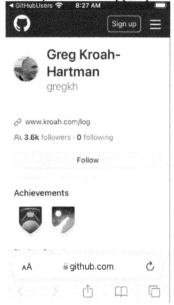

SwiftUI provides a dedicated *Link* view that opens a URL in Safari when pressed. You just have to provide the destination URL.

Adding Search to the App

We are currently hardcoding the search term in the request to the API to 'greg':

```
func getUsers(){
    if let apiURL = URL(string:
        "https://api.github.com/search/users?q=greg"){
```

Let's now allow users to specify their own search term to fetch their desired GitHub users:

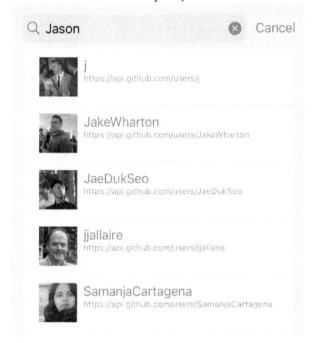

Add the following:

```
struct ContentView: View {
    @State var searchText = ""

    @State var users: [User] = []

    var body: some View {
```

```
NavigationStack {
    if users.count == 0 && !searchText.isEmpty{
        VStack{
            ProgressView().padding()
            Text("Fetching Users...")
        }
        .foregroundStyle(Color.purple)
        .onAppear{
            getUsers()
        }
    }
    else{
        List(users, id: \.login) { user in
            ...
        }
    }
}
.searchable(text: $searchText)
.onSubmit(of: .search) {
    getUsers()
}
}

func getUsers(){
    let trimmedSearchText =
        searchText.trimmingCharacters(in: .whitespacesAndNewlines)

    // Proceed only if searchText is not empty or just whitespace
    guard !trimmedSearchText.isEmpty else {
        return
    }

    if let apiURL =
        URL(string:
        "https://api.github.com/search/users?q=\(trimmedSearchText)")
        {
            ...
        }.resume()
    }
}
}
```

Code Explanation

```
struct ContentView: View {
    @State var searchText = ""
```

We have a state variable *searchText* to store the user entered search term.

```
.searchable(text: $searchText)
```

SwiftUI's *searchable()* modifier lets us place a search bar directly into a NavigationStack [screenshow]. And we bind *searchText* to what the user enters into the search bar.

```
.searchable(text: $searchText)
.onSubmit(of: .search) {
    getUsers()
}
```

And when a user submits, it will call *getUsers*. In *getUsers*, we proceed with the API request only if the *searchText* is not empty:

```
func getUsers() {
    let trimmedSearchText =
        searchText.trimmingCharacters(in: .whitespacesAndNewlines)

    // Proceed only if searchText is not empty or just whitespace
    guard !trimmedSearchText.isEmpty else {
        return
    }

    if let apiURL =
        URL(string:
        "https://api.github.com/search/users?q=\(trimmedSearchText)")
        {
            ...
        }.resume()
    }
}
```

And we append the search term to the API request.

At the start, we also proceed only if the search text is not empty:

```
if users.count == 0 && !searchText.isEmpty{
    VStack{
        ProgressView().padding()
        Text("Fetching Users...")
    }
    .foregroundStyle(Color.purple)
    .onAppear{
        getUsers()
    }
}
```

And that completes our application. In case you got lost at any point, the entire *ContentView.swift* is reproduced below:

```
import SwiftUI

struct Result: Codable{
    var items: [User]
}

struct User: Codable{
    var login: String
    var url: String
    var avatar_url: String
    var html_url: String
}

struct ContentView: View {
    @State var searchText = ""

    @State var users: [User] = []

    var body: some View {
        NavigationStack {
            if users.count == 0 && !searchText.isEmpty{
                VStack{
                    ProgressView().padding()
                    Text("Fetching Users...")
                }
```

```
                .foregroundStyle(Color.purple)
                .onAppear{
                    getUsers()
                }
            }
            else{
                List(users, id: \.login) { user in
                    Link(destination: URL(string: user.html_url)!){
                        HStack(alignment: .top){

AsyncImage(url:URL(string:user.avatar_url)){response in
                            switch response{
                            case .success(let image):
                                image.resizable()
                                    .frame(width: 50, height: 50)
                                //.scaledToFill()
                            default:
                                Image(systemName: "nosign")
                            }
                        }
                        VStack(alignment: .leading) {
                            Text(user.login)
                            Text("\(user.url)")
                                .font(.system(size: 11))
                                .foregroundColor(Color.gray)
                        }
                    }
                }
            }
        }
        .searchable(text: $searchText)
        .onSubmit(of: .search) {
            getUsers()
        }
    }

    func getUsers(){

        let trimmedSearchText =
searchText.trimmingCharacters(in: .whitespacesAndNewlines)
```

```
            // Proceed only if searchText is not empty or just whitespace
            guard !trimmedSearchText.isEmpty else {
                return
            }

            if let apiURL = URL(string:
"https://api.github.com/search/users?q=\(trimmedSearchText)"){
                var request = URLRequest(url: apiURL)
                request.httpMethod = "GET"
                URLSession.shared.dataTask(with: request) { data, response,
error in
                    if let userData = data {
                        if let usersFromAPI = try?
JSONDecoder().decode(Result.self, from:

userData){
                            users = usersFromAPI.items
                            print(users)
                        }
                    }
                }.resume()
            }
        }
}

#Preview {
    ContentView()
}
```

Summary

In the chapter, we learned how to implement a GitHub User Search application by connecting our iOS app to the GitHub RESTful API to get the data of different GitHub users. We processed retrieved JSON data from the API using the *Codable* protocol and *JSONDecoder*..

Chapter 6: Publishing your App on to the App Store

Welcome to the section where we're going to upload an app to the App Store. As illustration, we'll be submitting our Todo app we created previously in this book. But you can of course submit your own apps.

We will walk you through the necessary steps to prepare your app for the App Store. You'll learn about entering the required metadata, app icon and other details.

Running your Apps on a Device

Let's first see how to run our apps on a physical device. You can do so with a developer account with Apple (both free/paid).

Although it is technically possible to deploy apps on a phone wirelessly over Wi-Fi. I recommend using the tried and tested way of using a physical cable (i.e. lightning cable or USB-C, depending on your phone).

Connect the cable to your phone and computer, then in Xcode, go to 'Settings':

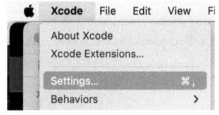

Under 'Accounts', hit the plus '+' button (bottom-left) and add your developer account.

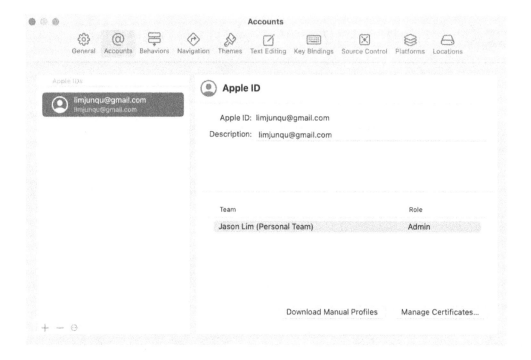

You can use either a free or a paid account for loading apps on your phone. However, to submit apps to the App Store or install them on multiple devices, you need the paid version, which costs $99 per year. We will discuss more about the paid account later on.

Once set up, you'll see options in Xcode to run your app on various devices, including your own phone. For instance, my phone is named 'Jason's iPhone'. Yours will display whatever you've named it.

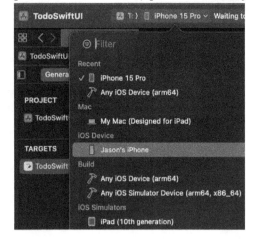

Select your device and hit run.

Xcode might prompt you to ensure your device is opted into 'Developer Mode':

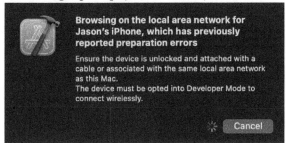

Just follow the instructions provided by Xcode and you should be fine.

When that's done, you can run your apps just like we've done in the Xcode simulator, and it will run the app on your device.

Uploading your App to the App Store.

Now, let's look at how we can upload our app to the App Store. Having your app on the App Store means you can share your app with the world. It's a significant step!

To get your app on Apple's App Store, you must join their developer program, which costs $99 a year. This fee allows you to upload as many apps as you like, not just iPhone apps, but also for Apple Watch, TV, Mac, etc. You get access to all their app stores for $99 annually.

Although the $99 annual fee may seem steep, it's immensely valuable if you're ready to showcase your app in the App Store.

A quick note: Apple might reject your app for a myriad of reasons (they will inform you). However, the experience of facing rejections and learning how to overcome them is worth it.

To begin, open up Safari (Apple's developer website works best with Safari). Go to *developer.apple.com*, and sign in with your Apple ID. You'll need to join the paid developer program and pay the $99 fee. Once you're signed in, you'll see a screen like this,

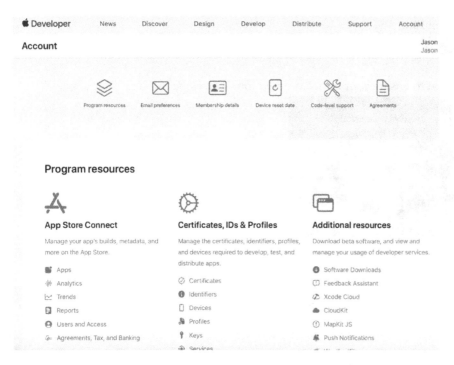

Here, you can download early access versions of Xcode, access certificates/IDs/profiles and many more.

Certificates, IDs and Profiles

Let's dive into some of the nitty-gritty details. This process isn't the most fun. It requires attention to detail, but remember that the goal is to get your app on the App Store and so long as we have this goal in mind, we can do this.

Under 'Certificates, IDs & Profiles', we'll create a certificate, an identifier, and then a profile (which is a combination of both certificate and identifier).

Program resources

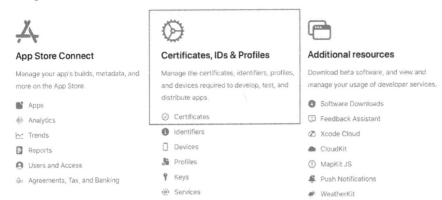

App Store Connect

Manage your app's builds, metadata, and more on the App Store.

- 📱 Apps
- 📊 Analytics
- 📈 Trends
- 📄 Reports
- 👤 Users and Access
- 💰 Agreements, Tax, and Banking

Certificates, IDs & Profiles

Manage the certificates, identifiers, profiles, and devices required to develop, test, and distribute apps.

- ⊘ Certificates
- ⓘ Identifiers
- 📱 Devices
- 👥 Profiles
- 🔑 Keys
- ⚙ Services

Additional resources

Download beta software, and view and manage your usage of developer services.

- ⬇ Software Downloads
- 💬 Feedback Assistant
- Ⓩ Xcode Cloud
- ☁ CloudKit
- Ⓜ MapKit JS
- 🔔 Push Notifications
- 🌤 WeatherKit

Start by adding a certificate. Click on 'Create a certificate':

Certificates, Identifiers & Profiles

Certificates	**Certificates** ⊕
Identifiers	
Devices	
Profiles	
Keys	
Services	

🔍 All Types ⌄

Getting Started with Certificates

Certificates identify who signed an app or is accessing a service. You'll need to set up various Apple-issued digital certificates to develop and distribute apps and connect to app services.

Create a certificate

Select 'Apple Distribution':

‹ All Certificates

Create a New Certificate

Software

Apple Development
Sign development versions of your iOS, iPadOS, macOS, tvOS, watchOS, and visionOS apps.

○ **Apple Distribution**
Sign your iOS, iPadOS, macOS, tvOS, watchOS, and visionOS apps for release testing using Ad Hoc distribution or for submission to the App Store.

This allows submission to any Apple store, including iOS and Mac. Select that option and continue.

Next, you will be prompted that you need a certificate signing request to show that its actually you (creating a certificate signing request can be tricky):

On your Mac, use Command + Spacebar to search for 'Keychain Access'. Click on 'Keychain Access', select 'Certificate Assistant', and then 'Request a Certificate from a Certificate Authority':

Enter the email address associated with your developer account and your name:

Leave the 'CA Email Address' field blank, choose 'Save to Disk', and save it to your desktop.

Be cautious with this certificate signing request:

The certificate signing request is crucial for updating your app and should be kept secure (it certifies that its you).

Once you have this file, return to the developer page, upload the certificate signing request, and download your newly created certificate.

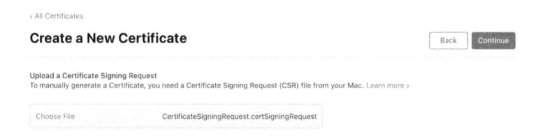

Click on the downloaded certificate, and add it to your keychain:

Remember that we are in the process of creating a certificate, an identifier and a profile. We have created our certificate and will next create an identifier.

Certificates, Identifiers & Profiles

NAME ⌄	TYPE	PLATFORM	CREATED BY	EXPIRATION
Jason Lim	Distribution	All	Jason Lim	2024/11/22

Creating an Identifier

Now, let's create an identifier, which uniquely identifies your app.

Certificates, Identifiers & Profiles

NAME ⌄	IDENTIFIER
Show Quick Quotes	com.greglim.quickquotes
XC com greglim furniture3D Furniture3D	com.greglim.furniture3D.Furniture3D
XC com greglim furniture3D Furniture3DUITests	com.greglim.furniture3D.Furniture3DUITests
XC com greglim HelloSwiftUI	com.greglim.HelloSwiftUI
XC com greglim helloworld TodoSwiftUI	com.greglim.helloworld.TodoSwiftUI
XC Wildcard	*

Add a new identifier by clicking on '+' (shown above), choose 'App IDs', and continue:

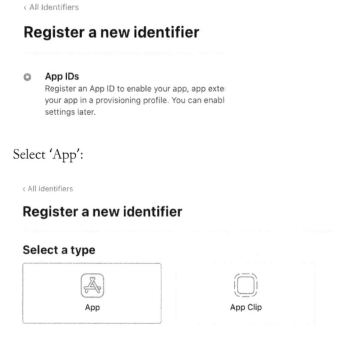

‹ All Identifiers

Register a new identifier

○ **App IDs**
Register an App ID to enable your app, app exte
your app in a provisioning profile. You can enabl
settings later.

Select 'App':

‹ All Identifiers

Register a new identifier

Select a type

| App | App Clip |

Enter an app description e.g. 'Daily Todos'.

‹ All Identifiers

Register an App ID

Platform
iOS, iPadOS, macOS, tvOS, watchOS, visionOS

Description
Daily Todo
You cannot use special characters such as @, &, *, "

Create a unique bundle ID, typically in the format 'com.yourwebsite.appname'. If you don't have a website, use a unique format like 'firstname.lastname.appname':

After entering these details, register the identifier by clicking on 'Continue'.

Copy the Identifier you just created (*com.greglim.todo* in my case)

In Xcode, under the target settings for your app, update the 'Bundle Identifier' to match the one you registered:

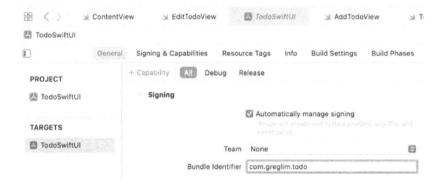

This ensures consistency between the app and the identifier.

Create a Profile

Finally, create a profile by combining the certificate and identifier. Go to 'Profiles', 'Generate a profile'

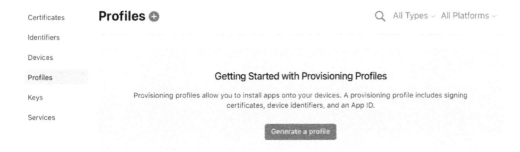

and choose 'App Store' under distribution:

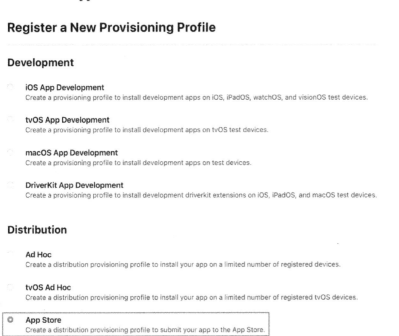

Follow the prompts to select the App ID and certificate you created.

< All Profiles

Generate a Provisioning Profile

Select Type > **Configure** > Generate > Download

Select an App ID

If you plan to use services such as Game Center, In-App Purchase, and Push Nc
to a single app, use an explicit App ID. Uploading apps to the App Store require
wildcard app IDs will no longer appear when creating an App Store provisioning

App ID: 7 App IDs

Daily Todo (8Y8H59JVBJ.com.greglim.todo)   ✕ | ⌄

Name the Provisioning profile clearly, e.g. 'Daily Todo iOS AppStore', and download it.

< All Profiles

Generate a Provisioning Profile

Select Type > Configure > **Generate** > Download

Review, Name and Generate.

The name you provide will be used to identify the profile in the portal.

Provisioning Profile Name

Daily Todo iOS AppStore

Type
App Store

App ID
Daily Todo (8Y8H59JVBJ.com.greglim.todo)

Certificates
1 Selected

With the certificate, identifier, and profile set up, return to Xcode. Ensure you have the updated signing settings with your developer account:

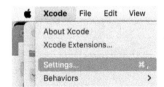

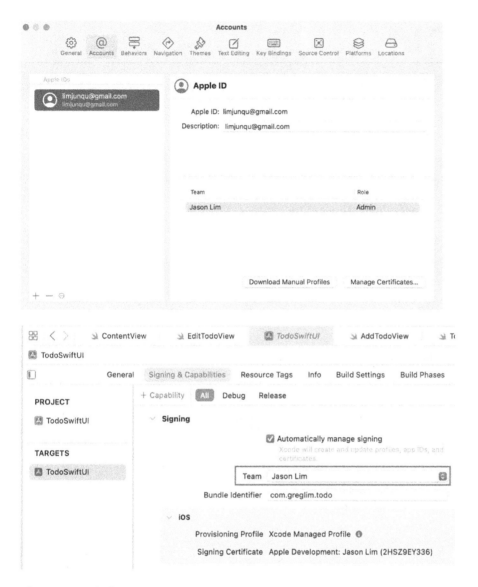

Creating an Archive

Before submitting to the App Store, do a 'Clean Build Folder...' to ensure readiness.

Then, archive the app:

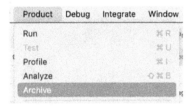

Although you could start the submission process now:

We have to first address missing elements like the app icon. We will do that in the next section.

Till now, you might find the steps to prepare your app for submission tedious. But it will make more sense as you do this for multiple future apps. Let's continue moving forward.

Uploading

Before uploading other assets, ensure that under 'Minimum Deployments', you have selected the correct iOS version (e.g. at time of this book's writing, latest version is iOS 17):

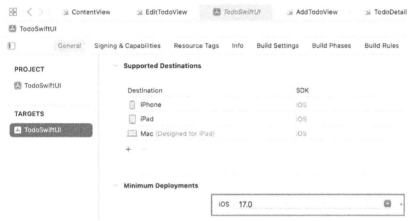

In this book, we've made everything for iOS 17. Technically, you could go back to iOS 16 or 15, but that would require certain code changes (eg. SwiftData is available only in iOS 17). So I recommend sticking with iOS 17. You may see updates like iOS 17.1, 17.2, etc. In these cases, I generally recommend using the latest version to maximize compatibility.

App Icon

Let's move over to our assets. Click on 'AppIcon' in 'Assets' where we have to specify a 1,024 by 1,024 px app icon.

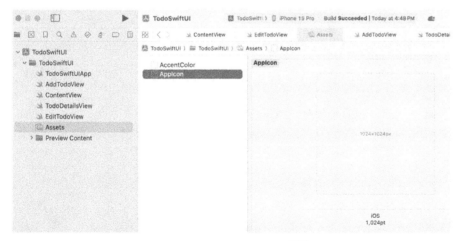

When creating your icon, remember it must fill the entire square without any rounding or transparency, as Apple applies these effects. Below, I have a sample Todo app icon that I generated using canva.com:

After generating your icon, in Xcode, drag and drop the icon into the slot.

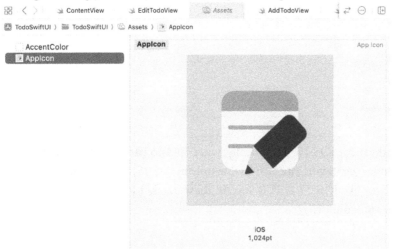

Once your icon is set, you can proceed to build and archive your app ('Product', 'Clean Build Folder...', 'Archive', and you're ready to distribute the app.

App Store Connect

In App Store Connect (appstoreconnect.apple.com), select 'My Apps':

Click on '+', and select 'New App':

Fill in the details for your app:

Now back in Xcode, click on 'Distribute App':

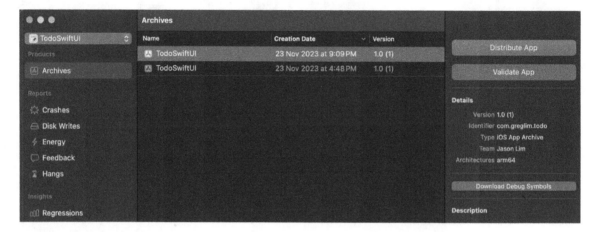

Select 'TestFlight & App Store':

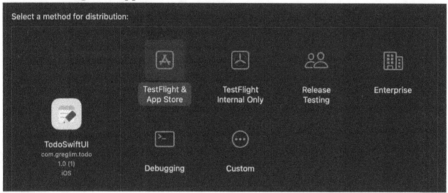

It will use 'App Store Connect' for distribution. If all goes well, you will get a successful notification.

You might encounter errors with certificates or app signing etc:

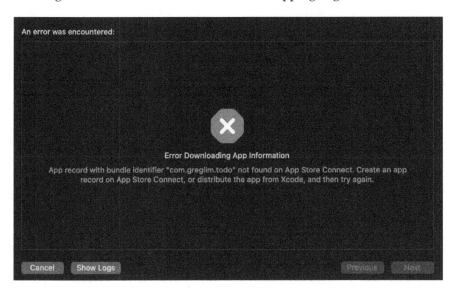

If that happens, try Googling the error messages and you should be well on your way.

Metadata

Once we have submitted our build to Apple, we move back into the App Store Connect page.

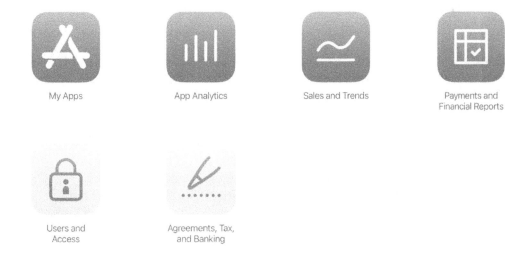

Navigate to 'My Apps', then go to your app.

At this point, you'll need to fill out a lot of information about your app, eventually reaching the stage where you can submit it for review.

For iPhone screenshots of your app:

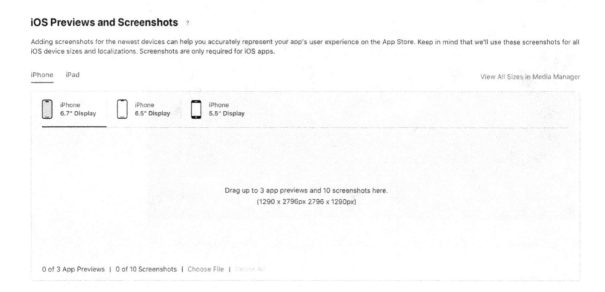

The simplest way is using your simulator. Run your app on a simulator, hit Command + S to save what's happening on the simulator screen as a picture, which you can then upload.

Next, enter your app's name:

App Information

This information is used for all platforms of this app. Any changes will be released with your

Localizable Information

Name ?

Daily Todos iOS

Subtitle ?

Consider how your app's title and subtitle helps in App Store optimization (akin to search engine optimization), which helps your app show up in search results. The more keywords you can fit into your app's title, the better.

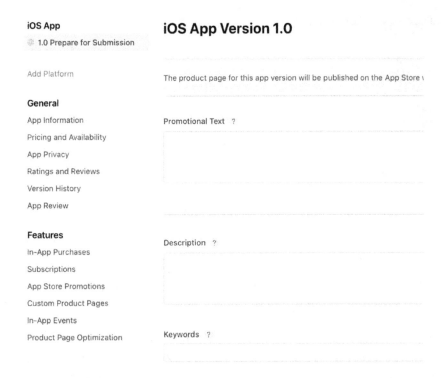

Fill out the description, promotional text and keywords fields (the *keywords* field is especially important).

When you reach the build section, you can select a build from your app, provided it has been successfully submitted via Xcode previously.

You'll see options for specifying if your app uses encryption, advertising identifier etc. And you should be on your way to successfully submitting your app for review.

Be patient with the approval process. It can take anywhere from a few hours to a week for Apple to respond. Most first-time submissions get rejected, so be prepared to make necessary changes and resubmit. The outcome can also depend on who reviews your app, so don't get discouraged by initial rejections.

Summary

We have gone through quite a lot of content to equip you with the skills to create an iOS app and submit it to the app store.

Hopefully, you have enjoyed this book and would like to learn more from me. I would love to get your feedback, learning what you liked and didn't for us to improve.

Please feel free to email me at support@i-ducate.com if you encounter any errors with your code or to get updated versions of this book.

If you didn't like the book, or if you feel that I should have covered certain additional topics, please email us to let us know. This book can only get better thanks to readers like you. If you like the book, I would appreciate if you could leave us a review too. Thank you and all the best for your learning journey in iOS development!

About the Author

Greg Lim is a technologist and author of several programming books. Greg has many years in teaching programming in tertiary institutions and he places special emphasis on learning by doing.

Contact Greg at support@i-ducate.com